THIRD-WORLD DIPLOMATS IN DIALOGUE
WITH THE FIRST WORLD

STUDIES IN INTERNATIONAL DEVELOPMENT
RESEARCH

Also published

Howard Richards: THE EVALUATION OF CULTURAL
  ACTION

Further titles in preparation

THIRD-WORLD DIPLOMATS IN DIALOGUE WITH THE FIRST WORLD

The New Diplomacy

ROBERT J. MOORE
formerly High Commissioner for Guyana to Canada

M in association with
INTERNATIONAL DEVELOPMENT RESEARCH
CENTRE

CENTRE DE RECHERCHES POUR LE
DÉVELOPPEMENT INTERNATIONAL
OTTAWA

First published 1985 by
THE MACMILLAN PRESS LTD
London and Basingstoke
Companies and representatives
throughout the world

Printed in Hong Kong

British Library Cataloguing in Publication Data
Moore, Robert J.
Third-World diplomats in dialogue with the First World.
1. Diplomacy
I. Title
327.2   JX1662
ISBN 0-333-36341-8
ISBN 0-333-36342-6 Pbk

To Alyma

Contents

Preface

The 1981 summit meeting at Cancun in Mexico was an admission: an admission that, although the North–South dialogue has so far been abortive, the need for recognizing the interdependence of the two sides was as great as ever.

Not much has come so far from that meeting. The consciousness of the danger inherent in the disparities between rich and poor was strong in some of the representatives of the North. But the will to turn that consciousness into action that will lead to a reordering of the world's systems to relieve the poor of their burden has yet to be summoned. The apologists of the rich nations often say that the problem of political will lies not so much in the leaders as in the led. Ordinary citizens will not appreciate any international structural overhaul that implies changes in their accustomed comforts. It is, at bottom, said to be a constituency problem.

Leadership, by definition, means a capacity to open new vistas, involving new opportunities, to those who are led. But it takes a high quality of statesmanship to look beyond the next election. When that quality of statesmanship exists, it takes an educated section of public opinion to give it the support needed. There must be a constituency sensitive enough to read the vision aright and communicative enough to make it acceptable to a fair part of the public.

Some political leaders may help create such a constituency, but their efforts alone will not bring it about. That is the work of men and women who reflect and research, of those who seek to interpret the world to their fellows and their fellows to the world, of those who educate the next generation, and of those whose beliefs take them from the immediate to the ultimate – all these are needed to create support for leaders who think both of the next election and of the next generation.

There are in every Western society men and women deeply

concerned that such constituencies be created. To them it is a
matter of life and death, for they are the representatives of the
nations wherein most of the world's poor live. It is their professional duty to negotiate for changes that will permit their
countries and their people to escape from the trap of underdevelopment. Diplomats by profession, they are usually expected to
operate within narrowly defined guidelines laid down when the
world was a very different place.

Of course they will be the first to point out that since the end of
the Second World War diplomacy has bifurcated into two types:
the traditional and the public. The former is the domain of the
professional diplomat proper; the latter that of a range of
different people. The one is expected to be quiet, subtle, avoiding
controversy and seeking smooth solutions by smooth methods.
The other is clamorous, controversial, even bellicose, and its
exponents seem to delight in the acerbities of partisan debate,
wars of words and explosions of national self-righteousness.
Traditional diplomacy is symbolized by two urbane figures
having a discreet chat over cocktails in a corner; public
diplomacy by the declamations of the United Nations General
Assembly or the voluble broadcasts, insistently dogmatic, beamed
to the citizens of other states.

But there is a third type of diplomacy, neither traditional nor
controversial but expository. Here the Third-World diplomat
seeks the formation of constituencies responsive to a future world
united by mutual interest. This study is an exploration into that
third kind of diplomacy. It is offered as a stimulus to a discussion,
in which there are many voices to be heard from, about the effective use of such a genre and the continuing refinement of its
methods. Not only is such a discussion necessary, but it should be
broadened into a much larger enquiry about Third-World diplomats, on whom very little has yet been written. True, some of
them are relatively new on the world stage, like the sovereignties
they represent. But the tremendous assignments given them –
assignments getting heavier as the twentieth century grinds to its
close – suggest that more thought be devoted to their prescribed
duties, their selection and training, the images they project and
their psychological responses to the burdens they bear.

Because of the very nature of the subject and the consequent
indelicacy of being too specific, this study has proceeded by way
of generalization. The author is aware that, as a witty Frenchman

has put it, 'generalizations are unavoidable, but like a politician elected by only a narrow margin they should be taken as valuable for only part of what they represent'.[1] However, the broad approach complies with two canons: one methodological, the other diplomatic. According to the first, in exploration one must always be tentative. According to the second, in diplomacy one must always be discreet.

Acknowledgements

This book would not have been possible without the generosity of the International Development Research Centre for whose award of a fellowship I wish to thank the President and the Board of Governors. I owe a special debt of gratitude to the Director of the Fellowship and Awards Division, Mr. J. Allan Rix, and his able staff, particularly Mrs Louise Rohonczy, Mrs Jacqueline Bustos and Mrs Fleurette Faubert for their unfailing courtesy, professional assistance and personal kindness.

I consulted a large number of people, too numerous to mention by name, all of whom I wish to thank. But I am particularly indebted to those Heads of Mission in Canada and elsewhere who went out of their way to put information at my disposal and to give me the benefit of their experience; as did the officers of the foreign ministries I visited whose patience was as gracious as their observations were helpful. Francine Gaudreault of IDRC typed the final draft, showing a tolerance of illegibility which was wonderful to behold. My daughters Fauzya and Lilah were, as daughters usually are, refreshingly helpful in their criticisms and suggestions. My son, Rayad, relieved me of many distracting chores. Alyma, my wife, was legendary in her patience; without her support this book would never have been completed.

Finally, I wish to thank the Government and people of Guyana for offering me the opportunity to observe diplomatic life from the inside, thereby creating an awareness of which this book is the outcome.

1   The Global Context: Vision and Division

The decade of the 1980s may well be seen in retrospect as the one in which humankind was compelled to make fateful decisions. Certainly it has begun ominously. People differ as to the reasons, but they are all agreed that the universe is not unfolding as it should.

The symptoms of *malaise* are obvious and inescapable. Once again, nuclear bluster is in the air as the United States and the Soviet Union entrench themselves in adversarial positions that many thought had been abandoned with the passing of the 1960s. Concern with *détente* has been replaced by concern with deterrent.

Massacres, like the one in Beirut, can still occur, leaving a tinderbox region of the world dangerously close to flare-up. Two nations, both in the throes of profound economic perplexity – Britain and Argentina – can go to war with the lethal accuracy of computer-controlled instruments over crumbs of land in the South Atlantic.

On the economic front, the picture is similarly dispiriting. The have-nots of the world, now numbered in the billions, are seeing the little that they *did* have close to the vanishing point. The haves can no longer be certain that the plenty to which the last thirty years of prosperity had accustomed them is part of the natural order of things. Uncertainty, as it has done in other periods of the world's history, is making them less disposed to take a larger view of their problems.

The crushing debt that now plagues the economies of many Third-World societies – Mexico being just one example – also plagues the economic thinking of First-World planners. Repudiation by the former could mean tremendous convulsions for the latter.

Where there is debt there is often hope – to keep creditors from losing their cool and debtors from losing their reason. But hope, once a commodity more in evidence among the poor than the more material commodities of food and shelter, has withdrawn before the bleak blast of the global economy. That is understandable. After all, the 1970s were described by the United Nations as the 'second decade of development'. As a description, it has gone the way of all great misnomers, for the substance of things hoped for has not become the evidence of things done. A better description of those years would have been 'the decade of galloping disparities'. Some development did take place, but it was not fundamental enough or fast enough to save the poor from getting poorer.

In this atmosphere of general perturbation, there are voices that cry out for 'global vision', meaning by that the positive will to see world problems as symptoms of a world-wide *malaise* that demands remedies more far-reaching than national ones.

These people say that all the forces working against the larger view can be summed up in two words: 'complacency' and 'procrastination'. Complacency, they say, is grounded not just in the negative force of indifference, but in the positive force of conviction. It is the belief that, although the universe does not seem to be unfolding as it should, there is a regulating mechanism – a hidden benevolent force – that will soon set things right. A comforting doctrine for those already comfortable; as an irreverent wit has put it: 'proof that heaven helps those whom heaven has already helped'.

Procrastination is seen as an even more subtle disuasion to action. It is the art of delay turned into a philosophy of life. Its practitioners argue that the problems are grave, but they do not argue that the time to tackle them has come. More needs to be known before anything fundamental can be done. Urgency is the enemy of clarity.

Third-World ambassadors, certainly those from the smaller and poorer countries, cannot agree with attitudes of complacency or proposals for postponement. They and their governments are convinced that time is running out; they feel it their duty to communicate this conviction to the peoples of the developed societies.

There is a truth, unfortunately not yet universally understood, that the comfortable cannot ignore: the patience of the poor has begun to run out. Millions in the Third World no longer regard their condition as ordained by God, fate or any other inscrutable but irresistible force.

The gap between the rich minority and the poor majority continues to widen. The haves and the have-nots are so far apart, physically and psychologically, that until recent decades no sense of outrage has arisen. Today the reverse is true. The vast poverty curtain certainly divides the developed from the developing, but it does not obscure. For the age of massive divisions among men is also the age of mass communications between them. At no point in human history have those who have had it so good and those who have had it so bad had so much knowledge of each other.

In previous eras, the rich and powerful created a mystique that justified and secured their overlordship. A mystique consecrates the holders of high position and great possessions as a people apart from their fellows. It sustains domination without explaining it. It gives mystery to mastery, putting the fathomable beyond analysis. Those imbued with it are made to seem, if not unapproachable, at least invulnerable. To what may be recent, it attaches the illusion of blue-blood lineage; to what could be changed it ascribes the power of immutability.

Mystique has often been used to create a belief in divine sanction or historical inevitability: the rich and powerful are the chosen instruments of the deity if the thinking is religious or of the momentum of history if the thinking is secular. Most important of all, the order of the world is made to seem *their* order, and an attempt to overthrow it would result in divine displeasure or social cataclysm, either of which would bring disruption but not change. Revolutions, it is claimed, may put down the mighty from their seats, but they do not exalt the humble and meek.

On a global scale, the mystique of the rich has been the chief casualty of the mass media. The cheap transistor radio, being as mobile as its owners, goes everywhere with them, filling their waking hours. Bombarding them with information as well as entertainment, it sells them attitudes. From the earliest days of independence, the rhetoric of equality preached by political leaders has been with them day and night. But so also have been the soap operas and other serials, which not only reflected the comfortable lifestyles of developed societies, but made them the pattern for the hopes of listeners.

The cinema is not as ubiquitous as the transistor, but it none the less is a powerful medium. It appeals to the eye more than to the ear, and for the illiterate or semiliterate, it offers an even more satisfying and rounded experience than the transistor, with effects considerably more enduring. In the last thirty years, most films shown in developing countries have come straight from the West. This medium made the comfort of the affluent visibly familiar. Familiarity bred not, as is classically affirmed, contempt, but discontent.

But most potent has been television, which combines some of the mobility of the transistor with the visual impact of the cinema. Most Third-World governments did not regard their independence as complete without a television network, not because, as some like to claim, it was a conspicuous status symbol, but because they saw it as an essential instrument in nation-building. It would inform and educate, and it would induct the diverse, sometimes centripetal groups within the new nation-states into homogeneous units.

But television can be as powerful in its disappointments as in its impact. It is a gargantuan consumer of talent, and to supply it with enough local material proved beyond the resources of all but a few developing countries (India for instance). Quickly there arose an embarrassing paradox: television in independent countries became increasingly dependent on programmes from outside. Outside meant, in fact, mostly Western countries, whose commercial suppliers were only too happy to stimulate a vastly remunerative market.

As television sets and hours of viewing multiplied, so too did the influence of the imported programmes on the conscious and subconscious minds of the viewers. The 'box' undermined deep-rooted attitudes of acceptance and resignation. It became a relentless agent of change: a revolutionary inflamer of appetites, enlarger of expectations, diminisher of patience.

It could be all these things because it put the poor in intimate contact with the bedrooms, boardrooms, showrooms and even classrooms of the affluent. It showed people jubilantly wasting the substance of the earth while they (the viewers) wasted away from lack of it. It posed the question, however inarticulate: 'If they can have so much, why must we have so little?' A surfeit of soap operas exposed them to plush grande dames, beefy business barons, opulent, rebellious adolescents, slick, crime-busting play-boys with their nubile nymphs – all devoted to orgies of a sensual, culinary, commercial or criminal kind.

All this soap did what soap is supposed to do. It helped wash away the fatalistic notion, encrusted on the psychology of the deprived, that their lives have to be nasty, brutish and short. What had displaced religion as the presumed opiate of the masses had rapidly become their awakener.

Curiously enough, religion itself, dismissed by Marx and his disciples for its tranquilizing effects of the poor, has turned out, at least since the mid-1960s, to have the very opposite effect. The self-immolations during the Vietnam holocaust were a portent. Buddhist monks, from being prayerfully passive in the face of the horrors of that war, found in their religion a stiffener to resistance. Protest became their ethical imperative. Even if the form it took seemed to secular, Western eyes curiously futile, it was an announcement of a fundamental shift in the attitudes of an apparently quiescent faith to the political crudities in its midst.

Soon, the centre of agitation shifted from Buddhist to Muslim areas. The decolonization of North Africa and the Middle East, Pakistan and Indonesia, gave the adherents of Islam there not only a new pride of nation, but a restored pride of religion. Islam ceased to be a religion of subject peoples and became a religion of sovereign ones.

For a while, it is true, its adherents remained content with that achievement, not seeking to disturb unduly the world's economic order or its continuing domination by the West. But Israel and the *jihad* against it stimulated more critical approaches to Western hegemony, and in some cases the approaches deepened into radical ones. Then came 1973, when the sovereignty of oil and the sovereignty of Allah reinforced each other. The sovereignty of oil, becoming increasingly pervasive after that year, began a shift in the world's alignment of power. The sovereignty of Allah, becoming compellingly evident as that change gained momentum, reached its high point with the overthrow of the Shah of Iran in 1979. The OPEC action was a unilateral form of indexation, challenging the long supremacy of the West in manipulating the prices both of what it sold and what it bought. The overthrow of the Shah, a revolutionary and religious action, indicated a much more profound change in attitudes, not only to Western military and political dominance, but to the international and national orders that dominance sustained.

Within Islam itself, upheavals are taking place. Increasing numbers of Muslims are convinced that submission to the will of

Allah does not enjoin submission to the vast inequalities between man and man within nations and between country and country. Religious ferment, never quite absent from Islamic societies, has touched off social ferment, itself not uncommon in Muslim experience – there have been repeated attempts down the Islamic centuries to recapture the egalitarian purity and justice ascribed to the early caliphates.

It is no longer possible to ignore this ferment, nor is it easily contained, even by the more orthodox Muslim rulers. To save their dynasties or their authority or their state apparatus they are being increasingly compelled to set about tempering if not removing social and economic inequalities. Condemning imbalances without, Islamic rulers are being forced by their critics at home to redress imbalances within. This in turn strengthens the voices of those who link all inequalities together, who call for a restructuring of the world's power system as well as its economic one.

Nor is Islam the only religion convulsed by social ferment. Christianity too has been experiencing movements of liberation, theological and political, particularly in Central and South America, and to a lesser but potentially great extent in the Caribbean and Africa.

In Central and South America, the Roman Catholic Church in particular has seen its followers take diametrically opposed views on political matters. Once it was securely wedded to the *status quo* either by material identity with it or by giving it the active blessing of approval or the passive blessing of silence. Now it numbers high-ranking prelates as well as humble parish priests who demand a change of structures in the name of greater justice for the poor. The theologians of Conscientization, a peculiarly Latin American school of thought, have been teaching the disadvantaged that their condition is eminently alterable. They teach that a consciousness of what makes them poor is the beginning of their liberation from poverty; that even violent revolution is not unacceptable to the God of the oppressed and that the elites that fatten off their misery are merely the local auxiliaries of an international political and economic order. These teachings are powerfully eroding the mystique by which the overlords of Latin America have preserved their hold on society for so long.

Most significant of all, in one stroke local injustice and global injustice are inextricably linked, and the removal of the one is seen as a necessary precondition for removal of the other. The overthrow of the Nicaraguan Somosa regime and its supporting elite is an index of the power and effectiveness of this kind of theological conviction. So also is the struggle still being waged in El Salvador. In both cases most of the revolutionaries take their inspirations less from the Communist Manifesto than from the Old and New Testaments – a threat indeed to any Latin American *status quo*, as Marx on his own does not, except in Cuba, have sufficient following to ignite change.

In the Caribbean, particularly the English-speaking part of it, the main-line churches, Roman Catholic and Protestant, have moved from an anguished concern for the misery of the poor to an active campaign for a change in the structures that make poverty endemic. They are vigorously pressing governments toward orders more egalitarian while emphasizing that human rights are non-negotiable. Although not calling for revolution to remove present political orders, they do advocate drastic changes induced by peaceful consensus within their societies. They too, like their Latin American counterparts, link local inequalities in the Caribbean with the global order. Any attempt to remove the former they see as a mandate to restructure the latter.

Elitism – ethnic, structural or economic – is seen in Africa as a local embodiment of an international disease, and there are signals that the resistance to it is not only gaining strength, but now gaining doctrine. Steve Biko was educated in the Christian tradition; he developed a theology of black resistance to apartheid that owed little to Marx, but drew on South African black experience in the light of the Christian ethic. Martyrdom canonizes not just the martyr, but his doctrine. And there are signs that the doctrine is acquiring powerful ramifications and moving across frontiers into Zimbabwe, Tanzania, Mozambique, Zambia and Zaire.

What renders all these developments – in Nicaragua, El Salvador, the Caribbean, South Africa and the Muslim countries – significant is their demonstration effect. Through the mass media all the world learns, however partially, however unclearly, about what happened in Nicaragua, Iran, Grenada or Zimbabwe. Change in one place touches off the impetus for change in others. For fallout is not limited to nuclear contraptions, but is now a characteristic of social upheaval right across the globe.

The upshot of all this is that chaos and uncertainty are now common in developing countries. Political leaders, at least the more realistic of them, are forced to take stock of what this phenomenon means. Their systems are at risk. They all realize this. Some invoke the police to stem the turbulence. Others realize that it is a problem not for police but for politics – politics of a new kind, in which their accustomed order will have to be refashioned in the interests of more people. Refashioning locally can only make sense if there is also international refashioning. That brings these political figures to the global approach, to the need to convince rich nations that, in Ramphal's celebrated phrase, 'not just the poor but all the world will be the poorer' if there is no peaceful change in the present international order.[2]

A brief look at what all this means is important here. The basis for any approach to international reconstruction is the awareness of its inevitability, whether men recognize this or not. The present crisis in the world's economic and political orders is *not* temporary. It is the result of a malfunctioning so grave and pervasive as to amount to breakdown. The list of current maladies testifies to this: global inflation, monetary instability, price fluctuations, the energy crisis, environmental threats and the escalating arms race. It follows that no national measures – such as protectionism, national or regional – can substantially alter the nature of the crisis, which is structural and institutional. In short, the fact that developing countries are doing very badly should not obscure the equally significant fact that developed countries are doing far worse than they ever anticipated. Both facts should together underline the third reality: that the present international economic order is doing no one a service.

The second basic consideration is that if international change is not smoothed by peaceful consensus, it will come by painful disorder. It will come by disruption, displacement and disarray, and the present imperfect orders will be replaced for some time by a jungle in which there is no order at all. This is too costly a prospect, especially for those whose comfort has become the non-negotiable basis of their existence. It is more prudent to give the inevitable a constructive direction than to leave it to take its own destructive path.

The third basic factor in these equations is that, if this Hobbesian state of nature is to be avoided, the rich nations must recognize the inevitability of sharing economic and political power with the poor ones – just as the elites of the poor ones will have to recognize the inevitability of sharing their economic and political power with the masses of their people.

In other words, what is at stake is an adjustment in the international balance of power. The euphemisms of conference vocabulary or the oblique language of diplomacy may obscure this reality, but it cannot be avoided by those nations that fondly believe they, on their own terms, can aid the developing world to an economic quasiviability without acknowledging the right of the poor to help make the necessary decisions.

Power shared inevitably means the acknowledgement of mutual self-interest. This is fundamental both to the peaceful evolution within national boundaries of social justice and to the peaceful reconstruction of the international system. The developed need the developing as much as the developing need the developed, but this is a fact widely unknown by the populations of developed countries, or, where it is known, widely ignored.

What the developed countries want, over and above a peaceful world, are an orderly rate of economic growth, full or near-full employment, uninterrupted supplies of vital raw materials and expanding markets for their outputs. What the developing world needs is the abolition of mass poverty in the shortest possible time, accelerated and equitable world economic development, equality of opportunity nationally and internationally and the right to take part in decisions on the future of a world in which their citizens form an increasing majority.

There is a point at which these two clusters of desiderata converge, and this fact is the key to a new international economic order (NIEO). Without accelerated development in the Third World indispensable raw supplies for the industrialized nations will be threatened, thereby seriously affecting their own growth patterns. If the Third World cannot sell its primary or industrial products, it cannot by the same token buy what the developed world produces. The richer societies will thus suffer the economic loss of an expanding market for their durable goods. If the needs of both sides are frustrated, it will make the world a tinderbox.

The coin has another side. The developing world needs transfers of capital and technology, which will not be possible unless the economies of the developed countries continue to grow. Further faltering in the rich countries means a decline in their demand for Third-World exports.

Ironically, recognizing that enlightened self-interest is a

mutual affair takes not just cerebral acuity but a higher quality: global vision – because the adjustments to be made on both sides involve short-term costs. These costs will be compensated for by the long-term benefits, but they weigh on the minds of Western politicians, who always have to think of the next election, and of the leaders of the developing countries, who will think of the resistance of their elites at home. As theologians say: 'Everyone wants to go to heaven, but nobody wants to die.'

Not surprisingly therefore, the negotiations that have been called the North–South dialogue produced little except sulphurous frustration and deepening cynicism. Yet the lessons of failure are usually more useful than the lessons of success – for success is always left to explain itself, but failure, especially for the victims of it, becomes the subject of prolonged reflection. A Third-World ambassador posted in a developed country should, for the better performance of his duties, carefully study this failure. The lessons to be learned can be summarized under two headings: the miscalculations of the South and the misconceptions of the North.

The major mistake of the Third World was to present the NIEO as a 'demand' of the South rather than the global need that it is, in that the existing economic order has not been working well. To get the NIEO accepted, it was essential first to engage the enlightened self-interest of the North, as the South had insufficient countervailing power with which to bargain.

The South was limited in its bargaining power because it had not thoroughly synchronized its objectives beforehand. Some countries were willing to settle for short-term concessions, others wanted long-term structural reforms. Unquestionably the South should first have had a great deal more South–South consultation to work out acceptable proposals covering the different interests of its constituents, albeit they were in substantial agreement about major objectives. President Nyerere's call for a secretariat of the South rigorously to formulate and co-ordinate economic proposals was wise and timely. It went unrealized and still does.

Many developing countries failed to appreciate the bargaining strengths they could have achieved through reforms at home to diminish inequalities between their elites and their masses. They also underestimated the extent to which the NIEO will depend on their own initiatives. Particularly they will need their own collective organizations to enlarge their economic power; they must then use the resultant countervailing strength to right the injustice that the international marketplace currently imposes on the world's poor.

But the North also made mistakes, just as serious as those of the South. With a parochial concept of global needs, it saw the NIEO as a need of the South that did not concern the North. It failed to see in the energy issue a symptom of a more universal problem to which, in common with the South, it is increasingly subject: the problem of excessive demand by a few wealthy nations for the dwindling physical resources of the globe. As a result, the North blocked all proposals by the South, not by directly denying their validity, but by producing myriad objections to every solution the South offered. Thus the *status quo* was defended by means of a stalemate.

The spokesmen for the North were concerned with immediate economic problems, which they wrongly assumed were eccentric breaches in the rhythm of their growth patterns. They largely failed to see how much the South was a part of the solutions to those problems, in that if for no other reason, the centre of demographic gravity now lies in the South. Not noticing the connection between their surplus capital goods capacity and the needs of the South, they preferred to try to solve their economic problems by themselves. Psychologically wedded to the *status quo*, the North, even where in some snaps of realism it recognized that a few structural changes were necessary, preferred the politics of procrastination to the politics of adjustment. The North's leaders were fearful of losing constituencies not educated to the imperatives for change. Their plea was that democracies are less receptive than autocracies to fundamental change, because democratic governments with an inconvenient degree of enlightenment are subject to the censure of the ballot box. Accordingly, they retreated into a narrow and insecure nationalism.

What the North really wished to perpetuate was the old dependency of the South, obscured by appropriate face-saving euphemisms. What the South failed to appreciate was that, in making its case, it should have built into the package the self-interest of the North and considered ways of reorienting the voting populations of wealthy countries.

Into this wasteland of international shillyshallying the report of the Brandt Commission came with freshening effect. Critics it certainly has, and many too. But certain features about it make it a climacteric document. First, the composition of the Commission was unique – distinguished citizens from North and South covering a wide spectrum of interests, including hard-headed finance people and passionate proponents of morality, activists for whom only the left offers justice, and thinkers for whom only the right offers hope; practitioners in the art of government and experts in the art of putting pressure on governments. So diverse a membership should almost certainly have guaranteed a lack of unanimity. But unanimity is exactly what the Commission achieved.

Nor was unanimity achieved at the expense of high-quality recommendations. The report could have been a cloud of semantic compromises resignedly put together to obscure the fact that a clash of convictions and interests had made substantial proposals impossible. But the central concept of a global community of peoples completely in need of each other's *wellbeing* informed the recommendations, giving them coherence and a very specific practicability.

Perhaps the most far-seeing aspect of the report is its insistence that a sustained, willed and reliable transfer of Northern resources would vastly enlarge the 'elbow room' within which *all* our disturbed and febrile systems have to work. This would in turn widen the area of choice (surely to a capitalist ear the sweetest music of all, as it multiplies the possibilities of alternative action without enlarging the risks).

But the.Brandt report is careful to consider the psychological barriers to the concepts it propounds and the measures it advances. The authors have no illusions about the resistance to change that governments of the Western democracies are likely to experience from their constituents; declares the report (p.63):

No matter how enlightened the plans for the economic and social betterment of people's conditions, they will achieve little unless in parallel the battle is fought at the same time in both North and South, to liberate people from outworn ideas, from the grip of narrowly conceived national interests and from the passions and prejudices inherited from the past. A New International Economic Order will need men and women with a new mentality and a wider outlook to make it work, and a process of development in which their full capacities flourish.[3]

On page 259 the authors take this line of thought a little further:

> The Commission considers it essential that the educational aspects of improved North–South relations be given much more attention in the future. It is imperative that ordinary citizens understand the implications for themselves of global interdependence and identify the international organisations that are meant to manage it . . . international institutions need to communicate for an audience wider than the community of persons which participates in their discussion and negotiations. Resolutions and declarations will only be effective if they influence the public at large. Youth and their organisations should be among the most important non-governmental organisations with which international institutions should intensify their contacts.

The report emphasizes that international organizations can help create constituencies favourable to international reconstruction. It does not mention the contribution diplomats from the developing world can make in this respect. This is an understandable omission, as the main concern of the report was with the motors of change. But diplomats can play a critical part, if they shed some of their notions of the essence and function of their profession and march forth from those privileged sanctuaries they so approvingly inhabit.

This, of course, is easier said than done. The weight of habit is against it, and professional habits, like personal habits, if they do not actually die hard, live resistfully. Indeed diplomacy, like the old-fashioned Roman Catholic priesthood, is one of the most conservative of professions.

But a leaf can be taken by Third-World diplomats out of the church's book. No institution in modern times seemed more impervious to change than the Roman Catholic priesthood, whether its members stood at the princely or the plebeian ends of the hierarchy. No institution in modern times has changed more remarkably or more profoundly. And the motive forces behind that revolution in concept, style and performance apply equally to representatives from the developing world. They can be summed up in three words: survival, dynamism, leverage.

2 New Wine, Old Bottles: the Tradition and its Limitations

As explained in the previous chapter, the Third-World ambassador posted to a developed country can contribute to a new kind of international politics. To do this he must shed some of the traditions of his profession. At the outset, therefore, he is subject to a sharp dilemma. Should he adopt the 'grand manner' at the risk of being untrue to his country's condition, or should he forego that manner at the risk of going unnoticed within the host country?

Yet this taxing dilemma is but a symptom of a more deep-seated problem: exactly what does he represent? And whom?

The first question seems almost tautological. An ambassador represents a national sovereignty. But – and this is more pertinent – he also represents a wider *urgency*, an urgency that he and his fellow ambassadors share alike. They do indeed represent the problems of their own countries. But collectively they highlight the malfunctioning of a global system. The urgency for which they press is therefore an urgency for change in the structures and arrangements of the globe. If they do not advocate international reconstruction their countries will have to employ other agencies in the developed world to do the job for them – an unwarrantable multiplication of costs to already overburdened economies.

And whom does he represent? The question seems also super-fluous. An ambassador is the servant plenipotentiary of the government in power in his country. Admittedly a sovereignty is an enduring entity (conquest and annexation apart), whereas governments are less so. But as long as a person is an ambassador he represents the government in power. If that government is a small elite, opulent, insensitive, exclusive and tenacious, set over the underprivileged, deprived masses, the change for which he presses in the international order bears no relationship to what he represents in his own country. But if he symbolizes the forces moving for change both globally and locally, he must consider how best to portray those forces.

This brings us back to the dilemma with which we began the chapter. Traditionally, diplomatic living has been grandiose. But the Third-World ambassador who conforms to such a lifestyle denies the need for greater equality in distribution of the earth's resources – which it is his professed duty to promote. His manner of consumption suggests a disregard not only of his own country's poverty, but also of the need for carefully husbanding the earth's resources.

Yet an ambassador cannot devalue the validity and dignity of the sovereignty he represents. In a world of nation-states the claims of dignity have so far been paramount, and there is a set tradition in the way they are asserted. Let us examine this diplomatic tradition from a historical perspective.

The nations of the West, in the old world and the new, have a number of traditions, one of which is that of the aristocrat. In some countries the tradition has an honoured and obvious place; in others it is understood rather than asserted. In the United States, for instance, the revolution ensured an absence of the titles and honorifics that in older societies connote an aristocracy. It did not ensure, nor was it meant to, an absence of the grandeur, material, attitudinal or political, that is the hallmark of patricians everywhere. And what was true at home was luxuriantly true for those sent abroad as diplomats.

As the United States moved from novelty to respectability and then to global supremacy, so the style of its ambassadors has matured. They have come to behave as to the manor born, radiating the aura of superstatehood. American diplomatic establishments may differ in tone and nuance from those of the old world, but not in magnificence. Few nations, other than those opposed in principle to capitalism, feel they could afford to have their ambassador to the United States deviate from the grandeur, hierarchical or architectural, of Washington.

In Eastern and Central Europe the kings and their courts have all departed. But in Western Europe nearly half the states remain contentedly monarchical. Where there is a constitutional monarch to make people feel stable, there too is a constituted aristocracy to make them feel vicariously privileged. Rather more remarkable, even in the republics the nobility continues to flourish. Hereditary titles and honorifics, it is true, are officially defunct, but members of the aristocratic families enjoy ample respect and influence within their societies.

The full democracy that has at last come to all of Western Europe has neither submerged nor obliterated the aristocratic tradition. The political philosophers of democracy have also found it too attractive to disparage. They have promoted the idea that the aristocratic ethos enshrines certain values that give maturity to the democratic polity. Inevitably, one of the areas in which aristocratic traditions and values are encouraged is the diplomatic service.

And not surprisingly. Senior European diplomats had for centuries been aristocrats; not always aristocrats born but frequently aristocrats created. The British have been particularly skilful in combining an aristocracy of birth with an aristocracy of merit or money.

Until after the Second World War, it was customary for Western European nations to send abroad as heads of mission members of aristocratic families. They were men to whom the etiquette of diplomacy came naturally and on whom complex and subtle responsibilities imposed no crushing strain. It was often assumed in Europe, even between the wars, that the salary and allowances of an ambassador would not cover his day-to-day expenses. No assumption could be more thoroughly patrician; serving the nation out of one's own purse in things political as well as social is the very core of this tradition.

Even where senior diplomatic posts were not staffed by acknowledged aristocrats, the incumbents rapidly became aristocratic by absorption. Officers rose in the hierarchy by displaying patrician qualities, the discharge of their duties and the exercise of their influence being conceived as impossible without them.

At the time this made sense. After all, it was a patrician world in which diplomats operated. He who was not at home in its traditions would stand out, his socializing with his counterparts being reduced to polite formalities. In short, he would be left out of the club, surely the most damaging thing to happen to a member of that profession.

In the United States, even if the untitled aristocracy did not always dominate the corps as did their titled brethren in the old world, it was none the less expected that recruits to the foreign service would practise correct behaviour and, by the time they had become seasoned professionals, act like patricians born.

Correct modes of behaviour were best ensured by giving preference in selection to those who had attended certain schools. Private schools (in Britain called 'public' by a characteristic quirk) were considered a better nursery of future ambassadors than state schools. They lived by the aristocratic tradition, emphasizing learning worn lightly, fitness pursued aggressively, finesse in social relations, wealth tastefully announced and collegiality sweetening competitiveness. Eton in England and Groton in the United States epitomize such schools in the Anglo-Saxon world. So with certain universities. Aristocratic values were considered, for instance, more inherent in Oxford and Cambridge than in Manchester or London. On the Ivy League campuses of the United States, the republican patricians had left their mark. Until recently in Canada, the alumni of a few universities – Trinity College, Toronto, Windsor, McGill, Dalhousie, Queens and Bishops – dominated the Canadian foreign service. If all were not ineffably patrician, they were comfortably elitist and where the one ended and the other began was largely imperceptible.

The justification for this practice was that in this type of work contact is as important as content. Wisdom is needed, but the ability to establish close connections with those who have information or power or both is crucial. To have already established them at school or university, where friendships tend to be enduring, was a qualification selectors could not resist. They argued that a diplomat would hardly cut a convincing figure in his posting unless he were in the confidence of his native elite. Without such friendships he would hardly be able to have his views heard or his recommendations respected at home. It was a circular argument, in a very charmed circle.

Since the ethos of diplomacy was that of aristocracy, it is useful to pause and consider this ethos.

According to its apologists, the aristocratic tradition brings to the cult of power – to be found in every nation-state – the discipline of good taste. Patricians are said to temper the crass self-seeking of acquisitive politicians and so preserve in politics a sense of principle.

As guarantors of a nation's heritage, they stand for continuity and stability. As the leisured rich, they can afford the time and money to set an example of public service. They can promote the arts and encourage more cultivated tastes among majorities. Sociability is their instinct, fine entertaining their *métier* and style their inherited aptitude. Hence, social graces and taste flow from them to those newly elevated to the ranks of the wealthy and powerful.

Aristocrats are a conservative class, although some members of it lean to the left, and by and large they work for a world of stately evolution rather than one of quickened change. But they are most at home in what Lord Rosebery, a late nineteenth-century British prime minister, called the Tom, Dick and Harry of politics, approaching problems by way of known, clubbable men with whom they can amiably disagree and seeking reform through remedial rather than structural methods. Discretion for them is not just the better part of valour; it is the whole of it.

When the colonial territories began to achieve independence, starting with India and Pakistan in 1947, diplomatic orthodoxy had long assumed its shape. In Western Europe and North America, the new diplomats were expected to regard themselves as heirs to those traditions; they might be black or brown or something in between, but the old practices would remain intact.

The important thing for Western political circles was to induce the new breed of ambassadors to become proponents of Western economic and political beliefs, structures and procedures to their own governments. Like Janus, the Roman god whose head pointed in two directions, the envoys of the new states would be spokesmen of their countries in the West and advocates of the West to their countries.

The West, of course, was not alone in these calculations. The Soviets and the Chinese expected the same dual role from the new ambassadors accredited to them: they would speak to Moscow and Peking of their country's needs while persuading their own governments that the primary need at home was for reconstruction on Marxist lines. In that competitive era known as the Cold War, capitalist and communist countries measured their strength not by nuclear hardware alone, but by the number of new states acceding to their faith or their alliances.

It was as much national self-interest, then, as it was the reverence for tradition that made the established nations encourage the new ones to adopt their manners and style. That is why the ambassador of a small developing country posted to one of the Western capitals was then, and still is, faced with a tradition the costs of which place a heavy burden on his government.

But that tradition is not the only problem such an ambassador faces. There is also the consumer ethic. In Europe since the end of the 1950s and in the United States since the end of the 1940s, there has been unprecedented growth (now rapidly coming to an end) in the economy, featuring a splurge of spending by all but the very poor. Consumers were programmed into wanting more and more. It was assumed that the more they spent, the more buoyant the economy became. Consumption, to vary the old adage about justice, not only had to be done, it had to be seen to be done. Thus competitive purchasing (facilitated by extended credit) constituted one of the chief social aims of society.

The ambassadors of the newly independent states arrived in the Western capitals as the consumer ethic was reaching its apogee. The confluence of the aristocratic tradition with this new social and economic mood meant that heads of mission had to act both as aristocrats and plutocrats. The ambassador was expected to possess the personal grandeur of the old order and the display of wealth of the new one. His car must be a thing of magnificence; all his appurtenances had to be plentiful and special.

In societies that have come to value people and institutions more by the image they project than by the reality, ambassadors from the new sovereignties – and even from some of the older sovereignties of Latin America – felt they counted for little unless their image was glittering. A high profile, as the media put it, was needed to keep one's country on the map. This seemed too often to involve a dash of manner and a splash of funds.

In this the ambassadors were to some extent reacting to what they thought was expected of them. The splash at first seemed legitimate, but by the time men had begun to realize there was no direct relationship between independence and prosperity, diplomatic sumptuousness had become a habit.

One of the most salutary facets of diplomatic life gives impact to these pressures: the relationship between protocol and actuality. Protocol decrees that all sovereignties are equal. Its intricate procedures ensure that the mighty and the weak, the immense and the minuscule, the well-known and the barely known, are accorded the same formal treatment by the host government. But there remains the reality that some nations

carry greater clout than others. Equality of recognition does not
mean and has never meant equality of influence with, or of access
to, the wielders of political power. What it has meant is the
stimulation of the small and the poor to compete for influence.
But influence is based on factors that have nothing to do with
ritual equality or lavish expenditure.

The extent of one country's influence in another can be the
result of many factors. First on the list is superpowerhood, and
following closely is power that is less than super but still considerable. Next comes economic, particularly industrial, strength
with strategic importance in tandem. Membership of the same
alliance, defensive pact or economic union carries almost equal
weight to those just mentioned, as does a shared ideological
outlook, especially if it is underpinned by physical proximity.

Sometimes a country enjoys great prestige in another for
historical or cultural reasons, like Spain in the Latin American
states or, supremely, France in Francophone Africa. Occasionally
the personality of an ambassador rather than the geopolitical
importance of his country is a source of influence. Of course all
relationships can change as new forces come to prominence.
Diplomats are taught to look for the shifts that can increase or
diminish their clout in the capitals of their posting.

In the first flush of the independence period, the new countries
were concerned that the recognition accorded them be exactly
the same as that accorded to the older sovereignties. Protocol in
the Western capitals ensured precisely that. But equality of
recognition is one thing; equality of influence is another. All the
suavity of protocol could not disguise the discrepancy between the
two, especially as the more influential states of Euro-America –
and for that matter of the communist block – regarded the arrival
of the new sovereignties on the world stage as merely increasing
the number of their clients.

The problem of achieving influence where it mattered
remained for each nation-state to settle. How the early ambassadors went about it now remains for us to see. But in order to set
their efforts in perspective, we must pause a while to consider the
social psychology of decolonization, which profoundly affected
their attitudes and behaviour.

The imperial systems, as the peoples of Asia, Africa, Oceana
and the Caribbean knew them, were systems of imposed inferi-
ority. Independence therefore not only created a new political

order, even more important it delivered people from a psychological incubus. Consequently the symbols of independence were as important as its political machinery. New nations naturally had to begin by emphasizing their rediscovered equality with those who had been their masters or those who, having no empires of their own, remained convinced of their own ethnic mastery. The outward and visible signs of racial equality were essential both to national self-esteem and to accustoming the older, white societies to the living fact of non-white nations in their midst. Among the emblems of sovereignty and racial equality, ambassadors came high on the list.

Conveniently so too. For an ambassador is both symbol and functionary, and the expense of the symbol could at least be justified by services rendered. Like the flag, the coat of arms, and spanking new parliament buildings and the muscular national stadium, the ambassador stood for an identity recovered, a history restored, vitality released, a people recognizing itself. In short, he represented both a state and a state of mind.

But his position in this respect was peculiar. Unlike governors-general, non-executive presidents and constitutional monarchs, his functions were not limited to ceremony. The rituals that surrounded him, the parties he gave and the appearances he made were one side of his duties. But there was the other side – hard negotiating, cautious and delicate representation, timely and subtle communications. These duties were to loom ever larger as time went on. At the beginning, however, of the era of independence, the ambassador's presence was more important than his substantial activities. He answered a psychological need of his people. It is not surprising that in the initial euphoria some nations overused this living symbol. For example, Ghana opened eighty missions immediately after independence and has since had to spend time and tact reducing them to a more supportable number.

A major aim in any nation's foreign policy is to create confidence in the stability and viability of its political and economic systems. Whatever else an ambassador may do, if he fails to inspire political and fiscal confidence in his government, he will not be worthy of his post or his pay.

Not surprisingly for Third-World ambassadors in the 1950s and 1960s in North America and Europe, this meant two things. First, the ambassador needed the magnificence that implies the same stability and assurance of those known to possess these attributes in the host society. Second, the ambassador must establish an easy familiarity with the governing classes of the host society, and to achieve this (so it was thought) his lifestyle and performance should not significantly differ from those of the governing classes. In short, he must become a member of the club, and that to most new ambassadors was a far from unwelcome condition.

There were other pressures. Traditionally (in some quarters still currently), diplomacy has been a competitive enterprise. Even where one country has joined with others in some type of organization (trade, defence, regional or whatever) it usually sees its role as unique in the undertaking. Common aims do not rule out competition; within the bounds of the organization they often intensify it. This was to be the experience of the new countries as their ambassadors appeared in the capitals of the older nations.

As the first of the new sovereignties were joined by others and settled down to the problems of government, the cult of symbolism began to melt into the quest for substance. The equality of states had to be cashed in terms brutally fiscal and economic; sovereignty had to be translated into power. Faith was to be justified by fact.

The leaders of the developing countries had expected that the end of empire would mean the beginning of a new world order. That order would have two characteristics: the first, recognition by Europe (East and West) and North America that the earth now had other centres of gravity than their own; the second, that the older nations would willingly help the new ones to their feet in the interests of a stable world. These expectations were quickly dashed and that in turn had an important bearing on the role of Third-World ambassadors.

If a new world order was their aim, the political elites of the emerging states thought that their countries deserved some compensation for the mistakes of the old one. The prophets of decolonization attacked imperialism on the ground that it had arrested the natural evolution of their societies and warped their development. They argued that it drained away the wealth of their countries to the metropolitan centres, because it allowed to flourish only those sectors that bolstered the economic and political power of the empire as a whole. Imperialism had also stunted the growth of initiative and talent.

So independence was seen as something more than free-dom; it would, with the transfer of state power, multiply the opportunities local hands could grasp. To make the New Day possible, the political leaders considered massive aid necessary. It was a moral obligation on the part of the old imperial powers, not merely because they had it to bestow, but because it was a form of repatriation. According to the new rulers of these societies, the erstwhile mother-countries had founded their prosperity and economic hegemony on the sinews and sweat of the colonies. Now the time of reckoning had come for restitution. Independence meant not that the former masters were free of responsibilities and obligations, but that new obligations were imposed upon them, particularly the duty to help make the economies of the new states healthy and resilient.

But the sources of aid were perceived to be wider than the old centres of empire. The United States was known to have an interest in decolonization. Not only was it congenitally hostile to formal empires, but also it expected free countries would allow a free penetration of their markets by American commerce. The American desire to secure the opportunities provided by the new nations was matched by the new nations' desire to secure American aid. One good turn deserves another. Finally, by the end of the 1950s, helped to its feet by Marshall Aid, Europe was once more becoming an economic giant. Having lost its role as the centre of an empire, it found one as a central emporium of goods and services available to the new nations, possessed of the will to make its influence felt in those quarters once again.

To the dismay of the leaders of African and Asian countries, aid did not prove automatic – a sobering discovery for the more sanguine of them. In that moment of truth they realized that to secure even a little of what they needed they had to offer substantial *quid pro quo*s. For the pie was smaller than the recipients expected. They were made to feel that to increase the slice of any one nation meant diminishing the slices available to the others. Adroit bargaining became essential and inevitably they competed among themselves. Those ambassadors whose countries were strategically critical to the Western alliance or blessed with natural resources vital to the Western economies did not have to strike too high a pitch to attract the required flows. But those not so favoured had to use all their diplomatic finesse to induce the assistance their governments instructed them to get.

They had to prove either an energetic obedience to Western interests or the threat of a left-wing takeover.[4] Or they had to ingeniously magnify the supposed benefits to the donor countries that aid to their own would bring. Admittedly, the principle of restitution was piously recognized by left-wing parliamentarians in Britain, France, Holland and Belgium, but governments gave it short thrift.

In fact the Cold War was better than contrition at opening coffers. From the end of the Second World War to the interlude of *détente*, the East–West conflict dominated the thinking and strategies of Western governments and their advisers. In the combat of ideologies, aid was a powerful weapon – a palpable persuasion to the rulers of Third-World countries to keep the Russians, Cubans and Chinese from their doors and admit only the pure and orthodox as their advisers and co-workers.

But aid, though supposedly an insurance against red revolution, had its limits even for that great reservoir, the United States. Spending on arms, for instance, always took priority over spending on aid. Accordingly, the urbane and unceasing competition common to diplomats of the old school became also the norm of the new. If anything, competition became even more acute and flamboyant. For the rise of the new states coincided with the rise of new aspirations among their inhabitants. Ambassadors were the predictable targets of these aspirations, for by common consent they existed to induce that flow of goods and services without which independence could have no substantial meaning. The breadth of influence achieved by a Third-World ambassador in the capital of his positing thus began to be seen as crucial to the economic viability of his country.

If influence was the talisman of aid and aid was the test of an ambassador's effectiveness, then those means believed to create the magic spell had to be fully exploited. Here, the combination of aristocratic tradition and consumer ethics made captives of the envoy. Intellect, however tremendous, would not suffice. Neither would negotiating skill. Style was indispensable. At this point, the diplomatic reasoning ran along show-business lines: a talented performer is useless without a stage.

The new ambassadors set the time-honoured stages. They entertained – opulently – the powerful, the near-powerful, the clearly ambitious and the consciously fashionable. Obviously the setting must do justice to actor and audience. But style, that most

elusive of theatrical talents, became confused with sumptuousness, and the stage threatened to eclipse both the actors and the
script. Not for the first time the medium had become the
message.

Thus the cult of splendour, already assumed to be mandatory,
led to the cult of largesse. It was confidently assumed that the way
to a cabinet minister's heart was through his stomach, or at least
through his liver. This, the gastronomic theory of influence,
became dogma, and its new believers rejoicingly multiplied. Nor
did Western politicians and bureaucrats noticeably resist this
doctrine. After all, diplomatic cultivation was to them not so
much flattery as a pleasing recognition of entitlement. All this
meant that it was not enough for the ambassador's residence to be
baronial, or his automobile to be ducal. His entertainment must
be regal.

A platitude has it that the whole duty of an ambassador is to
build bridges between his own society and the one to which he is
posted. Bridges the new ambassadors certainly came to build, but
they were frequently of caviar, and the liquid that flowed beneath
them was champagne. This kind of operation still has authoritative advocates. But fortunately it is no longer an unquestioned
doctrine, and its critics are found both within and without the
charmed circle of diplomacy.

Lavishness also was in theory justified because to many it
demonstrated that the country was a 'going concern'. Investment
was conceived as the other side of the aid coin. To attract enough
to boost the economy under acceptable terms was the hallmark of
a good ambassador. It was contended that investment depended
on assuring the multinationals and other would-be investors of
the stability of the country, the reliability of its government and
its immunity from or ability to cope with sudden disruption. Part
of the day-to-day skill of an ambassador and his staff was to
provide the necessary assurance. At the least they should create
interest and attract enquiries; at the most they would sustain the
negotiating process that would lead to investment.

Most fundamental of all, the function of the ambassador was to
persuade interested parties that the political elite of the state was
receptive to capitalist penetration. Whatever its rhetoric might
say to the contrary, he was called upon to explain, it shared the
same basic business ethic as the potential investors. Its lifestyle
was Western in orientation (even if local in nuance), and it read

journals like *The Harvard Business Review, The Wall Street Journal, The New Statesman* – with a slight cough of dissent – and *The Economist* – with a less-than-slight cough of assent. Assurance would best be given by an ambassador radiating Western sophistication, one at home in the approved clubs, who offered food and drink of the standard of a connoisseur.

This behaviour was based on assumptions about how development would come about that were widespread in the 1960s – heralded as the Decade of Development. The developing countries were expected to be brought into the modern world by following the steps that made the United States and Western Europe into industrial societies. According to this belief, all societies fall into five economic categories: the traditional society; the one ready for take-off; the one in the throes of take-off; the maturing society; and the final mass-consumer society. Whatever the history, structure, class formation or religion of a society, it would progress through these stages toward capitalism, private or state or a combination of the two.

Those who paved the road for this happy consumation would, of course, be the new elites, without whom a 'backward' society could not get into its stride. Complete with the 'proper' values from the universities of North America, Europe or their local surrogates, the members of the elite would assemble the capital necessary for take-off, which is another way of saying industrial revolution. The economy, under their leadership and drive, would broaden to the benefit of all, and the days of plenty would follow.

The multinationals, it was considered, would stimulate the emergence of a capitalist elite. These corporations would give a momentum not previously evident; establishing infrastructures to serve their own needs, they would also serve the needs of those with some capital. Expatriate corporations and local entrepreneurs would together create the conditions ripe for capital formation and thus for a burgeoning bourgeoisie. The economic thinkers of developing societies – at least those who looked to the West for inspiration – did not necessarily swallow the whole doctrine. But nearly everybody accepted it as a basis; industrialization became on all sides synonymous with growth, whether its proponents were capitalist or socialist.

This, the famous trickle-down theory, reached its high noon by the end of the 1960s. As the rich in each developing society grew richer, the argument ran, the poor would become less poor – the way to eliminate poverty was to pile more loaves on the rich man's table so that the volume of crumbs falling would steadily increase. If the future lay with the elites, those who represented them abroad must leave no stone unturned, no bottle uncorked and no cutlet uncooked to prove that they and their class were already in the mainstream of history.

The urge for magnificence was, of course, also personal; the grand manner suited the new envoys particularly well. Some were aristocrats, some tribal chiefs – people to whom spacious living came as readily as breathing. But whether they were old stagers or newcomers they had not been able to give full rein to their abilities in the days when their countries were ruled from outside. Many were men of the law who knew they were capable of advocacy or decision of a much higher, more testing sort than the bar or bench called for. Those with higher education had mostly been at Western universities: Harvard, Yale, Princeton, Oxford, Cambridge, St Andrews, London or the more elitist universities of France, Germany, Holland, Switzerland and Portugal, seats of learning that were patrician by circumstance or aspiration. These universities had been seen as levers of upward social and political mobility, but the return home was inevitably a terrible letdown. The coveted posts were in the hands of the proconsular class. The ceilings for capable local men were depressingly low, and even when they were raised, as they slowly were in some colonies in the half-decade before independence, the new levels often meant office without real power or titles without responsibility. An elite they might be by birth, education and residence abroad, but as long as their country remained a colony they were attendant on those whom empire had placed over them.

In the British Empire, they were not asked to be English in soul. But they were required to honour values dear to the heart of an English gentleman: constitutionality, commonsense, an urbane anti-intellectualism, gradualism and sportsmanship in games and politics. If they were subjects of the French Empire, their assimilation was expected to be complete. What was erroneously called a 'colony' was to the French an organic enlargement of France, as incapable of being separated from it as was Marseilles or Lyons. And those inducted into French civilization had no intelligent option but to be French.

This helps to explain a significant difference. Ambassadors for countries once part of the British Empire can usually put a distance, psychological, political, personal and cultural, between themselves and London, albeit they may be ardent members of the Commonwealth. Their Francophone counterparts find it difficult not to consider Paris as the hub of their universe.

Whatever empire a country formerly belonged to, independence brought not only top posts at home, but a range of postings abroad. As Basil Davidson has observed, 'The lucky few enjoyed it enormously, uproariously, above all extravagantly.'[5] Not unexpectedly, this enjoyment was observed at its height in the new diplomatic services. The aristocratic tradition of diplomacy prescribed magnificence; the consumer ethic required luxuriance. Why should diplomats deny themselves these entitlements both of a profession and of a prevailing mood, especially when it was their purpose to demonstrate not their country's 'backwardness', but its potential for 'modernization'?

In countries with a long-established diplomatic service, promotion to ambassadorships comes according to well-understood criteria: routine appointments within the foreign service, reward appointments for political figures and special appointments for distinguished professionals outside the foreign service. In the newly independent nations, as there previously existed no foreign service, the first crop of ambassadors were usually men and women who had contributed heavily to the independence movement. They could be pardoned if many of them saw their appointments as a reward. Accordingly the perks of the job loomed as large as its travails. Black-tie dinners and gala receptions, in their eyes, made up for the toil, tears and sweat, sometimes even the blood, that were the price of leadership in the independence campaign. In the early postcolonial experience, governments did not protest their ambassadors' expenses. That would come later as the intangible benefits of diplomacy were set off against the tangible asperities of budgeting at home.

These compulsions of tradition, economic mood, symbolism, persuasiveness and personal satisfaction all converged to render the diplomatic style of most Third-World countries in the first decade – in some cases in the first two decades – after independence as patrician and sumptuous as (sometimes even more so) that of the older countries of Western Europe, North America and Latin America. But some Third-World countries had another reason for sumptuousness – their refusal to be part of the East–West conflict. They did not deny the reality of the conflict. What they denied was the need of their being part of it.

Because they were determined not to play the game by the same rules, they felt the style of their diplomats should not depart too obviously from tradition. They were not seeking isolation; they were encouraging reappraisal, and not for the first time a radical departure in international affairs had a conservative effect on diplomatic behaviour. Thus the diplomats of the leading non-aligned countries felt they could not afford to abandon the manners and procedures that give diplomats a common medium of exchange. The decision to be different in concept reinforced the resolution to be identical in style. Another great paradox of the diplomatic universe was in the making.

If the 1960s were for developing societies the decade of diplomatic magnificence, the 1980s are likely to prove the decade of diplomatic reassessment. By the mid-1970s it was evident that the rich had become richer and the poor poorer, and that the gap between them was widening at a horrendous rate. The glow of optimism had gone from most of the leaders of the developing world. On both sides of the poverty curtain, statesmen were noting that the first decade of development had yielded almost no results and the second was clearly going to yield only meagre ones. Growth there had been, but it was far less than expected and was totally lopsided – the increase in gross national product was matched by the increase in gross national inequalities.

A few in each society had done well, most had not, and this despite the continuous flow of aid, technical personnel and loans from the World Bank, the International Monetary Fund and private lenders. Considerable sums had been spent in developing countries by various United Nations agencies, but the results were vastly disproportionate to the expenditure of skill and money. The norms of most Third-World economies had come to include unfavourable balances of trade, tremendous indebtedness and a shortage of foreign currency.

Where foreign exchange is short, diplomatic services begin to be looked at with searching eyes. Even in one-party states, criticism has begun to be raised over the cost-effectiveness of diplomatic functions. Because so much of what a diplomat does is intangible, the profession is easier to criticize than to defend.

Ambassadors say that if anything goes wrong between two countries, they will be blamed, but if anything goes right, the ministers at home will take the praise.

1973 was a watershed year. Oil joined the expanding list of products whose prices had been rising over the previous three decades. What was called the first oil-price hike was given all the attention, critical or approving, normally reserved for a revolution. Which it was. For the products whose prices had been escalating were those the developing world purchased from the developed. There had not been any corresponding rise in the prices of commodities the developed countries purchased from the developing – until 1973, when it happened with a commodity the rich nations regarded as their lifeblood.

This reminded the wealthy of an ominous lack of equilibrium in the economic ordering of the world. It also showed the poor nations without oil deposits how vulnerable they were. The more they had to pay for oil, the more their reserves of foreign currency drained away, and the more they scrutinized all expenditures that dipped into their reserves. Examining their diplomatic services, they could come to no clear conclusion as to whether economies could be effective without damaging their utility.

More than ever, the poor countries felt they needed representatives among the rich, if only to remind the latter of the deteriorating conditions behind the poverty curtain. Cutting staff clearly offered a more feasible alternative to closing missions. But here the planners were up against the usual bureaucratic tendency. Most heads of mission make plausible pleas for more, not fewer, staff, explaining how the mission is doing a crucial job in an area of growing importance that, if not immediately visible, would shortly become evident. It is equally difficult for the financial bureaucrats at home to scale down the status symbols of ambassadors and their staffs. They too felt caught in a dilemma; although they recognize that ambassadorial grandeur is no longer economic, they hesitate to deprive their ambassadors of what they consider insurance against obscurity.

The older developing countries especially are reluctant to give up those baronial mansions, purchased early in the era of independence when prices were manageable, whose maintenance, particularly in cold climates, is now a serious headache. The fact that they are owned by one group of Third-World countries has stimulated others to acquire equally impressive residences. The newer arrivals have had to bear the escalating costs of property in diplomatic enclaves, which have their own special rates of inflation.

There are those in the rich societies who criticize the opulence that still marks most Third-World ambassadors. Others, some of great standing, urge that such opulence, however unrepresentative of conditions at home, is indispensable. No doctor, they point out, is complete without his instruments. A persuasive, if inappropriate, analogy.

Over the last half-decade the critics have in fact been growing in number and becoming more vociferous. Since the special United Nations session on the new international economic order in 1974, the North–South dialogue has concentrated on the deteriorating economies and quality of life in the developing world. Those who attend or read about these conferences have started making the obvious observation: the lifestyle of ambassadors from even the poorest Third-World countries shows little recognition of the plight of those societies and makes no allowances for the burdens they place on the home economies. In short, the claims of diplomacy in a changed world must be seen in relation to the claims of humanity.

But those same people who see the dichotomy between ambassadorial opulence and the poverty of their countries admit to feeling short-changed if a diplomatic reception they attend is less than opulent. It takes courage to break so strong a tradition, and flair to get away with it.

And yet the poorer Third-World countries cannot go on maintaining high-priced missions. Increasingly the South (as the less-affluent parts of the world are now called) is engaged in strengthening its relations with itself. These new missions and new ambassadors are as crucial as those in Western (and Eastern) Europe and North America. For what they imply is much more and better cooperation within the South, and there are signs that this need is gaining recognition. But each new embassy in another developing country cuts into the money available for them all. Nor is it prudent to short-change missions in developing countries to sustain those sent to Europe and North America.

Realism, self-interest, a sense of balance and, increasingly, credibility demand that the lifestyles of ambassadors in the rich countries be brought into line with the realities at home and the other diplomatic needs of the home government. Ambassadors should not be expected to live so humbly as to render the job unattractive and the incumbent embarrassed. But it does mean that the legendary luxuriance has to be dispensed with, that caviar and champagne are unnecessary for serious dialogue with people of power and influence, that competitive lavishness should be replaced by cultural liveliness and that taste should take the place of display. After all, the representatives of the Third World must take their own case seriously. What they are asking for is global equality of opportunity, not global equality of opulence. The symbols they use must judiciously reflect the conviction.

3 Keeping the Global Perspective: Aids and Impediments

If the image of the grand seigneur is neither applicable nor affordable by developing countries, it is timely also to examine again the role ambassadors can play in the richer parts of the world. They are already performing their traditional functions: representing their countries' sovereignties; attracting notice and negotiating aid; trying to improve the terms of trade; defending their countries' reputations; and proving the legitimacy of their political institutions and the rectitude of their international behaviour. As the twentieth century nears its end, are these traditional functions enough, in view of the profound reconstruction now demanded by the developing world? The answer seems to lie not in denigrating the traditional functions but in putting them into new contexts. It is not premature at this point to consider what ambassadors can do to increase the receptivity of people in developed countries to a more realistic approach in the economic ordering of the world.

Ambassadors for small, Third-World countries, in redefining their functions for the 1980s, can begin by reviewing their *modus operandi*. They are asking the countries of the North to acquire a global vision. Then they too should possess the global perspective; to ask of others a catholicity of outlook and to be themselves parochial not only distorts their case, it diminishes their credibility. This means in actual practice that they have to know more about the workings of the international system than the average ambassador from the developed nations.

This is not impossible or unheard of. It has been done before. Let us consider an analogy from the developed world. Denmark, Finland, Norway, Sweden and the Netherlands are small in area and population and are close to historically ambitious powers.

Their security and the mastery of their own affairs have often been rather delicate matters. In addition, they speak their own exclusive languages that few foreigners have found worth the time or trouble to learn. These nations could easily have been cocooned in narrow, national isolation.

But their inhabitants have been healthily aware of these realities and have taken steps to manage them. Their educational systems heavily emphasize linguistics; they learn not only the languages of their neighbours but the main international languages – English and French, with Spanish not far behind. To guard their freedom of national action, they have also developed an intimate and extensive knowledge of the international system and have mastered the art of turning the intricacies of that system to their advantage.

They are internationalist by outlook. Dependent, one or two of them, on foreign trade, and superb linguists, they have refashioned the handicap of their smallness into a marketable virtue. They are found out of all proportion to their numbers and the size of their countries in significant, even key positions in all the important international organizations – thereby becoming a small sector of the world at the service of the world.

The achievements of these nations should be for ambassadors from small developing countries an inspiration and an incentive. The smaller the sovereignty, the greater must be the diplomat's knowledge of the world's system. First, because his country's vulnerability demands it, and second, because when he is putting his nation's case the roundness of his vison will make that case certainly respectable, arguably persuasive. If anything, he should know more about international developments than even the officials of the ministry of foreign affairs of the country of his posting. A specialist in one area he can certainly be, but he cannot afford to be a specialist and nothing else.

He will inevitably have to deal in specifics with mandarins and bureaucrats. That is what is expected of him, and his presence must ensure that those mandarins and bureaucrats have a fair idea of the immediate results of their country's economic and political policies on the country he represents.

What are the day-to-day specifics of a Third-World ambassador's job? He will spend more than a third of his time on promoting – or trying to promote – trade on acceptable terms between his country and that of his hosts. He will also spend large slices of time encouraging substantial aid flows. Also time-consuming but no less vital are negotiations for certain forms of technical assistance not big enough to be classed as national projects: construction of an airport hanger here, or a water-supply system for a farming community there, procuring a microfilm reader for a university library, building a bridge over a difficult river, and so on. To ignore these concerns is to sell his country short – and their list is often long. They are nitty-gritty indeed, being the satisfaction of immediate wants. Governments are pleased when their ambassadors relieve the pressures for community services or equipment by securing them as aid. Indeed all governments *expect* their ambassadors in developed countries to do this in addition to tackling bigger issues. Some Third-World governments go even further. They assume their envoys will plead special circumstances to extract special concessions and most-favoured-aid flows from the governments and agencies of developed countries. This requires each ambassador to portray his country as *sui generis*, a unique case deserving unique attention culminating in a 'special relationship'.

These matters are admittedly important. But there is a great danger that the Third-World diplomat will get lost in them to the prejudice of the global imperatives he now represents. He should remember he is an actor in a small part of a drama. The actor can only be effective if he has a thorough understanding of the drama as a whole and lets his performance be dictated by the total meaning and message of the play. Every aspect of the relationship between a developed and a developing country either confirms the present lopsided world economic order or contributes to the process of its dismantlement. This is a consideration that the ambassador must keep constantly before him; in serving the whole he will serve the needs of his own part – the country he represents. That is why he has to make it his business to know a great deal more about events right across the board than do his opposite numbers from the developed societies.

But to do this brings the ambassador face to face with three major problems – all closely interrelated: the problem of time, the problem of maintaining his global grasp and the problem of selecting data to strengthen it.

Ambassadors are busy people. A head of mission is responsible for the welfare of his staff, for the image of his mission and for the day-to-day representation of his country's position to the various ministries in the capital city of the host country. If his embassy staff is too few or not adequately trained, he will find himself doing more than his own share of work to ensure the effectiveness of the operation. On top of all this, he has to attend endless receptions, dinners, levees, soirées and all the sundry manifestations of obligatory socializing to which diplomats are, by the pressure of their peers, bound.

Diplomatic functions take up so much of his time that they actually militate against the effective performance of his duties, broadened as those duties are certain to be in the 1980s. Play the game he must, but he should not allow himself to become an enthusiast.

Let us examine precisely what burden normal diplomatic entertaining places on an ambassador's timetable. If, for instance, our ambassador is stationed in a developed country with eighty resident missions (and that is low; countries like the United States, Canada, Britain, West Germany, France and Italy each have well over a hundred) he starts with at least seventy-six national-day receptions to attend. Inevitably there will be four countries or so with which his own has no diplomatic relations, mercifully relieving him of four more receptions to think about.

With roughly one-fifth of the seventy-six, his country has only marginal contacts, and the ambassador need put in only half an hour's appearance. In a year he will have consumed a total of seven hours in doing so. The remaining sixty-one states can then be divided into two categories. With thirty-one of them, his country's relations will be cordial but not critical. Our ambassador is likely to spend one hour at the national-day reception of each country in this category, swelling his total of reception hours by thirty-one a year.

The next thirty countries will be important to his own in many respects and for many reasons. To demonstrate the warmth of ties, the ambassador will cheerfully spend two full hours at each of the national-day events, taking his total of hours in this category to sixty and his grand total of hours spent sipping cocktails at national-day receptions to ninety-eight.

But national days do not close his liquid innings. Taking the lowest possible figures, let us say that each of the seventy-six ambassadors hosts only four additional receptions per year. That amounts to 304 events to which our ambassador may be invited. If he attends only one third of these (which would be very abstemious of him) and scores an average of one hour at each, his total will amount to an additional 101 hours per year.

Every year sees the departure through retirement, reposting or promotion of some twenty of his colleagues, each of whom has a farewell reception. Assuming an average of one hour per reception, he will consume twenty hours in confirming the fraternity of the profession. Presidential or prime ministerial levees, visits of heads of state or government or the secretaries general of international organizations, red-letter days of the host country, climacteric events in government ministries or agencies, cultural events of command-performance variety – all these will require our ambassador to attend at least another forty receptions at which he cannot without impropriety spend less than an hour. These will add to the calculus of bibulation another forty hours of upstanding merit.

Diplomacy is reciprocal. A guest our ambassador will often be; a host he must be most frequently. He too will have a national-day reception, plus at the least four other receptions per year. At his own events he must stay the full duration, adding another ten hours to his roster and bringing the grand total to 269 or roughly thirty-three, eight-hour working days.

But cocktails are the small potatoes of diplomacy. Dinners are the thing. Heads of mission with vast resources host one dinner every week or even more. Some do it once a fortnight. Most middle-sized or small Third World states tend to manage one a month. Taking the last figure as a working average and remembering that our calculations are based on seventy-six missions, we will find at least 912 dinners occurring each normal year in the diplomatic circuit. If our ambassador attends only one-fifth of these, he will sit down to 182 of them. Tradition demands, and protocol emphasizes, that no guest at these affairs should leave before three hours have passed. Our ambassador will therefore have spent 546 hours in dedicated consumption of food and drink.

Government ministers and senior officials, members of parliament, heads of government agencies, heads of corporations and other eminent public figures also host dinners for diplomats. If our ambassador attends fifty of these in a year, spending the prescribed three hours at each, another 150 hours will be credited to him for diplomatic virtue. Hosting one dinner a month himself will bring the total hours spent in reciprocity to thirty-six. The grand total of all these hours spent formally at table or at cocktail parties amounts to 901, which is equivalent to 113 working days – so many days spent in the long littleness of diplomatic geniality!

Nor does the record of his obligations stop even there. As the ambassador's tenure lengthens and he ascends the pecking order of precedence, he will become better known and better appreciated. So the occasions demanding his presence will multiply themselves. Unless he is uncommonly disciplined he will find himself so swamped by these little rituals of the trade that he is able to surface for little else. To misquote a remark about a member of another profession: such time as he can spare from the adorning of dinners he may devote to the neglect of his duties.

When all this is accounted for, however, he is still not off the hook. More hours must be devoted to the twenty-minute courtesy calls that convention demands newly arrived ambassadors must pay. Sometimes that twenty-minute period proves excessive, caller and host spending the time in frantic, if urbane, search of something to say that treads the thin line between the politely inconsequential and the patently insubstantial. Wisely, some of the hosts, if the visitor hails from a small, not-well-known developing country, peep at an atlas beforehand. And there are those who prudently consult an encyclopaedia (up to date, one hopes) for salient details about the caller's country to convince him that his host possesses breadth of outlook and depth of fraternal concern.

If the two ambassadors are from countries with close connections, economic, ideological, political or organizational, the call usually goes along merrily for an hour or nearly two – not a waste of time, but time that could easily be spent at lunch rather than in a courtesy call. There is much discussion of these courtesy calls. Some say they are a waste of a busy professional's time; others assert they are an invaluable introduction. The tradition is certainly tenacious; many mock it but continue to conform.

Those who visit only some give grave offence to those left off the roster. But there is a way, surely, of honouring the tradition economically. Instead of having to visit all ambassadors individually, the new arrival could call on the most senior ambassador of a region, who by prior arrangement will have assembled his regional colleagues to meet the new ambassador. In this way, the caller will meet on average six of his colleagues every time he makes a courtesy call, saving him and them long hours of not-always-stimulating exchange, hours that Third-World envoys in particular could devote to more fruitful endeavours.

But there are other types of courtesy calls, not to be under-valued. They do take up a great amount of time, but it is time well spent. These are visits by the newly arrived ambassador to members of parliament, congress or whatever the nation's legislative body is called. His visit to the president or prime minister belongs to a different category, being *de rigueur* and therefore always arranged for him by the protocol department of the foreign ministry.

The ambassador will obviously call on members of the cabinet. Pacing his visits rather than rushing to see them all in the shortest possible time will allow him to do his homework on the various ministers, their policies, their hobby horses, their backgrounds and their outlook. In the introductory discussions the minister can elucidate the political life of the host society and the ambassador can deal with the proposals of the developing countries for international reconstruction and his own country's need for it. Such mutual enlightenment lays the groundwork for a continuing relationship.

Governments and Oppositions in Western democracies are likely to change places, a fact the new ambassador will remember when he visits the leaders of the Opposition parties, major and minor. He will learn how their philosophies, policies and timetables differ from those of the government and will explain his own government's positions on vital issues. Cultivating the Opposition without offending the incumbents is a skill no ambassador in Western countries should be short of, whatever his origin.

Where the political system calls for senatorial committees to examine the executive's policies, the Third-World ambassador will be on familiar terms with the chairmen and ranking members, especially of committees that deal with trade, aid, budget review, international finance and foreign affairs. He will find, to his surprise, that one of his *raisons d'être* is to remind such important people of his country's existence.

Further down the line, the head of mission will call on the civic dignitories of major cities, many of whom have connections with major international commercial enterprises. He will not omit the editors of leading newspapers and journals, paying particular attention to those amenable to international overhaul. Nor will he fail to call on the leading trade unionists of the nation, whose goodwill will be of immense value during his posting.

All this is necessary and salutory, often productive. But at this point there arise two weighty considerations no self-respecting ambassador can ignore. First, even though he cuts his attendance at cocktails and dinners to the minimum compatible with maintaining good relations with his colleagues, he will still find those occasions eating heavily into his time. Second, he will have to devise a system to keep abreast of situations on both global and local levels; he has to be fed with scholarly, politically sound analyses and assessments from research-oriented minds whose perspectives transcend the North–South dichotomy.

To the consideration of that system he will return. But let us look for a moment at an important aspect of the first problem: how can Third-World ambassadors make their entertaining more manageable and more meaningful?

There are three basic rules to guide ambassadors: first, entertaining in groups some of the time is better than entertaining singly all of the time; second, to be memorable a diplomatic function does not have to be expensive; third, it is wiser to give a few parties with imagination than many without it.

These rules have been successfully applied in some Western capitals. Obviously, many developing countries belong not only to global organizations but to regional ones – organizations such as the Andean Group (Junta del acuerdo de Cartagena), the Caribbean Community, the West African Economic Community and the Association of South East Asian Nations. A significant number of Third-World countries belong to the Commonwealth and a large number belong to the Non-Aligned Movement. Least known among the intelligentsia of Western nations are the regional organizations; the Non-Aligned Movement is somewhat better known but often woefully understood, while the Commonwealth, even among thoughtful people in its senior member-countries, is often referred to as the 'British' Commonwealth – an organization with which the present Commonwealth has only the most vestigial of affiliations.

Although ministers and high bureaucrats and some corporation executives, journalists, academics, religious leaders and non-government organization members know about these group-

ings and what they are doing, only a tiny proportion of the thinking strata of Western countries is aware of them. Most thinking
people, if they have heard of these organizations at all, have only
the haziest notion of what they are and are doing.

Clearly, the ambassadors whose countries are members of one
or more such associations have a duty to make them known. The
knowledge that they exist and function needs to be shared with
those who either wonder whether the Third World ever does anything to help itself or doubt the possibility of equitable
cooperation between developed and developing countries.
Receptions cohosted by groups of ambassadors are an effective
beginning to the process of enlightenment. Effective because the
act of communication – a party – is also an act of pleasure.

Such occasions have many advantages. First, the costs to the
diplomats involved bear little relation to the impact they have
and the contacts they make. Shared overheads will reduce the
bills each ambassador has to pay to more acceptable levels –
always good news to the envoys of poor countries with many
foreign missions to keep up.

Second, the process of organizing such events, involving as it
must close and sustained contact between heads of mission, often
turns formal colleagues into firm friends. The bond thus created
shows itself in further acts of solidarity in other areas of
diplomatic behaviour.

Third, ministers and the senior members of the government
and corporate bureaucracies are more willing nowadays to attend
a cohosted reception than those with single hosts. Predictably, the
tremendous rise in the numbers of Third-World missions has
resulted in the declining attendance of these officials at their
functions. They simply cannot spare the time. A reception hosted
by six or eight ambassadors gives them the chance to pay their
respects to several excellencies at the same time as well as to
honour the association they represent.

Fourth, if that kind of event is well orchestrated, it will attract
the media, who will focus their attention less on the reception
than on the regional or global group that is hosting it. This is all
the more likely if the guest list is wisely made up to include
eminent media personnel of known sensitivity to Third-World
issues.

This brings up the question of the invitees. The one thing
certain to defeat the point and purpose of such a party is having

too many guests. To invite, for instance, a thousand people to a reception hosted by eight ambassadors is, even making allowances for the non-attendance of one fifth of them, to swamp the diplomats and make it impossible for them to communicate. To invite 600 people, knowing that about 500 will show up, is to have a perfect number with whom to establish contact. But who are invited is as important as how many. Instead of inviting the whole diplomatic corps (which would leave little room for others) the dean could stand as their representative. Besides cabinet ministers and their mandarins and commercial figures with broad international interests, the list should concentrate on leaders of thought and opinion in the country – parliamentarians interested in development, top trade-union officials, leading editors, educationalists (including those who direct the writing of textbooks), academics with interests in developing countries, officials of the various institutions that deal with international affairs, representatives of industrial, technological and agricultural federations, officials of advertising agencies, and youth leaders who have shown an interest in and a flair for international affairs. Such people are all, in their various ways, communicators. They will spread the knowledge they have gained to their associates, and they will make further contacts with the diplomats they have met.

Food is one of the most stimulating introductions to the cultures of others. The lack of it for millions of poor people is one of the most unsatisfactory features of the global economy. Third-World ambassadors, when they entertain, should keep these two propositions in mind. Through the kinds of food they serve they can quicken their guests' interest in their societies. Through the quantities they serve they can tacitly demonstrate how to avoid wasting it.

These two principles were successfully tried more than once in an experiment in Ottawa, Canada, in the late 1970s. The high commissioners of Commonwealth countries there decided to celebrate Commonwealth Day by cohosting a dinner to which each mission (some 19 of them) contributed a main dish and a dessert characteristic of its country. The result was a rich culinary and educational experience for the guests – 225 of whom were invited. They were treated not only to a menu with a range almost as wide as the world itself, but also to the folkdances, the poetry, instrumental music and songs of the contributing countries.

Varied as the dishes were, there was an economy about the amounts of food served – an object lesson to those who feel that diplomacy and waste go together. The media each year gave full coverage not only to the dinner, but to the Commonwealth as well. In addition, because many people across Canada wanted to know how to make the dishes, a recipe book was published – a work of collaboration between the high commissioners and the Canada Department of External Affairs. This exercise in creative co-operation between representatives of sovereign states should be parallelled by other associations elsewhere.

The annual national-day reception has become such a fixed rite in the diplomatic universe that it seems almost sacrilegious to suggest that it is not necessary to hold one every year. Yet there may be considerable wisdom in staging bi-annual celebrations especially for those countries chronically short of foreign exchange.

But financial considerations apart, there are good reasons for this change of routine. The aim of such a celebration is, or ought to be, to remind the invitees of both the country's existence and its essence. That aim is not well served, if served at all, by a reception that is almost identical with those of other countries. It will have no impact on the guests, most of whom are veteran members of the cocktail circuit.

To be memorable, a national-day party has to be distinctive, and that demands time to plan, patience to gather material from home and imagination to arrange. Are there any useful guidelines for shaping it in the national interest? Three come to mind: first, it should combine some of the functions of an exhibition with the delights of a party. Second, it should have a theme. Third, it should when necessary be used to correct, delicately of course, misconceptions about the home country that are being purveyed in the host country.

Paintings, artefacts and pieces of sculpture – potent creators of atmosphere – are invaluable for projecting the required images. So too are photographs and transparencies, telling their story as they do adroitly, colourfully and noiselessly, attracting the eye but not dulling the conversation.

There is no difficulty in finding themes – a country's scenic beauty, its flora and fauna, the range of its people, their culture and subcultures, its architecture and its development thrust. To choose a theme that chimes in with a prevailing mood in the host country is a sure way of kindling interest. For instance, ambassa-

dors from multilingual and multicultural societies stationed in
Canada in the 1970s – when that country was deeply concerned
with bilingualism and multiculturalism – would have stirred
Canadian minds if they arranged their displays around those two
themes. 1976 and 1978 were important years in the United States
and Britain respectively (the bicentenary of the American
declaration of independence and the 25th anniversary of the
accession of Queen Elizabeth II). Those Third-World ambassadors who projected aspects of their countries' histories at the
national-day receptions would make friends for themselves by
cashing in on the prevailing historical interest.

Finally, a national-day exhibition can counteract the media's
tendency to present one-dimensional images of foreign peoples. A
guest at a Nigerian party confronted with the superb bronzes and
masks of that country would realize that there is more to its way of
life than the politics of oil. Where a group of university students
from home exists, an ambassador, drawing on their talents and
performing skills, can offer guests dancing, singing and music for
their edification and entertainment. If the guests have something
to *see* as well as to drink, they will remember the former and perhaps forget the latter, and the cause of developing countries will
be well served.

I shall mention one last experiment that deserves a wider
usage. A few missions have begun providing portraits of their
countries – presenting their societies in a way that neither the
media, academia nor travel organizations can do, but using some
of their techniques.

A day is set aside (usually a Saturday), and the invitees number
only about 25. The country is introduced by short talks, transparencies, films, books, paintings, sculptures and artefacts. Two
typical meals – at midday and at the end – are provided, with
menus explaining their preparation, nutritional content and cultural or religious origin and significance. A fashion show depicts
the range of clothing and jewellery, and there is singing and
dancing. The event lasts for about six hours; it is aimed at media
people, prospective visitors, members of parliament, filmmakers
and teachers. Embassy staffs and volunteers have shown enthusiasm for projects of this type.

If Third-World ambassadors can bring to their social lives both
the perception and the imagination that their situations require,
they must have more time for the other demands placed on them.
To this problem we must now return.

The Third-World ambassador is a medium with a message. To be sure, he is other things as well, and they cannot be minimized. However, he has a paramount aim. In the decade of the 1980s he has a duty to get across his global message to differing levels and widely ranging groups in the country of his posting. Obviously he must first get the message himself, and that involves having a substantial background of thought on which to draw: a conceptual framework brought constantly up to date with fresh material as the push and pull of global forces affects its substance. In short, he must get his thoughts in order and establish for himself a doctrine of what he wants to do and how he wants to do it.

No medium can be effective unless it is clear what is to be conveyed and to whom. The latter is as important as the former. The message must be sensitive to the thought processes – verbal, intellectual and symbolic, inspirational and moral – of those to whom it is addressed. Otherwise the seed, however vigorously and widely broadcast, will fall on stony ground.

This means that the ambassador must immerse himself in the *weltanschauung* of the society. He must be aware of the sacred cows and the fashionable and archetypal symbols. He should learn what are the prevailing economic dogmas and the economic realities. And he should pay special attention to the words or symbols that evoke passionate hostility or enthusiasm. Acquiring this sensitivity takes time, observation, analysis and reflection.

Most important of all, the Third-World ambassador must constantly seek areas of common interest between the position he represents and the society with which he is holding a dialogue. Detecting these areas calls for profound thought, an exercise not readily compatible with the airy chitchat of cocktails and the elaborate opacity of representational dinners.

But this is to run ahead. Let us go back to the ambassador's first requirement: the conceptual framework mentioned above. This background of thought and knowledge has to be strengthened and reinforced at suitable intervals, and those intervals should never be allowed to become long. Conceptual frameworks are not, as every ambassador knows, frozen entities. They are daily being tested by events, experiences, new political configurations and new social and economic forces. But a framework there must be, global in its dimensions if national in its location, to give coherence to the ambassador's many activities and decide the priorities of his embassy's outreach.

A valid conceptual framework provides the ambassador with a

doctrine to regulate his activities. He thus can proceed according to plan, checking his progress over a given time. His overall strategy will be defined by the ministry of foreign affairs and the ambassadors' conference; the conceptual framework will enable him to judge the most efficacious tactics. It is vital for his country and for his own satisfaction to have a yardstick to measure his achievements. For his country the importance is twofold: first, achieving some of his objectives will validate at least some of the conceptual framework and perhaps lead to its further refinement; second, the failure to achieve other objectives will cause a foreign ministry to review the tactics or strategy used. In both cases the country's foreign policy will benefit.

On the personal level, being able dispassionately to assess achievement and failure is excellent for the ambassador's mental hygiene. It avoids one of the worst *malaises* of diplomatic life: uncertainty – the haunting sensation that one cannot really tell what effect, if any, one is having. That condition induces a discomfiting sense of weightlessness, the compensation for which is a passionate intensification of formal gaiety. The ambassador in question convinces himself that high visibility is a proof of personal magnificence, and personal magnificence is a proof of professional efficiency.

Should the ambassador adopt that line of reasoning, he may incline to set greater store in his dispatches by phrases like 'as the foreign minister said to me at dinner last night' rather than by a critical comparison between the *sotto voce* 'confidence' and the minister's actual policy. For the Third World, an envoy more masterly at the round table than at the dinner table is better than one whose virtues are the other way round; of course it would be a bonus if he were equally masterly in both contexts.

Being clear about objectives makes diplomatic socializing manageable for three reasons: first, one knows where and with whom things will get done; second, one knows where to relax; third, one knows to which events one can safely sent the deputy.

A few paragraphs earlier I posed the question of how can an ambassador keep abreast of the global scene. Let us return to this problem. One way to ensure this, particularly for a small developing country not encumbered with numerous missions, is an annual conference at headquarters for all ambassadors. At first sigth this seems impracticable if not preposterous, and the objections to it do deserve notice. By any standards it is expensive, by some standards it can be unwieldy and by some foreign services it is deemed completely unnecessary. After all, its detractors will say, ambassadors are fed with gargantuan quantities of material from home. Indeed they are bombarded with tons of paper, some of it confidential, all of it informative, to keep them fully conversant with developments at home. If they diligently read all that comes to them they have no need of an annual conference.

But there is the rub. Can an ambassador read and digest all that comes to him from home as well as all that comes to him from the various information mills of the country where he resides? Can he easily relate the two? How can he get through the many journals and reports issued meticulously month after month that purport to analyse the currents of international affairs – the shifts of policy in Whitehall or the White House, new lines of thought or action in Peking, Riyadh, Brasilia or Jakarta? If he did all that and did it thoroughly he would spend all his time reading, which is precisely what the nature of the job, as we have seen, prevents him from doing. For one of his functions is to interpret for the policymakers at home the currents of the society where he is posted. His other function is to present convincingly the political decisions and positions of his own government to the policymakers and opinion formers of his host country. In addition to all this, he has to keep a broad, indeed panoramic window on the world in order to understand the pressures operating on the two societies he is relating to each other, and to observe their reactions.

Of course his staff will do some of the reading for him and prepare digests of the relevant publications. But a wise ambassador will read the most important documents himself, even if he reads them selectively. Interpretation is not just a matter of applying acuity to printed material; it is a matter of bringing to bear one's experience on the thought and decision-making processes of others. In this the ambassador will usually have the advantage over the younger and middle-ranking members of his staff.

To do all this, an ambassador needs an annual occasion where he can get together for in-depth, private discussion with his colleagues in an atmosphere that is democratic in procedure and global in perspective. Just as there are times when one picture is worth a thousand words, so there are times when one discussion is worth a hundred written reports. It is a source of humour among ambassadors that foreign ministers hardly ever read long dispatches. I once received the apocryphal advice, 'for a dispatch to be immortal it does not have to be eternal'. But those who follow such advice and keep their dispatches short may find themselves rebuked for being 'impressionistic'. There is a classic bureaucratic dilemma here: length is trusted, unadmired and largely unread; brevity is encouraged, enjoyed and largely suspect. The received wisdom is that length, because it is assumed to be carefully researched and copiously supported, is an accurate guide to the current situation on which the ambassador is reporting. Brevity, by seeking to distill rather than to detail, is an accurate guide indeed – but merely to the ambassador's selective hunches. There is a further irony. A long dispatch is usually read by a desk officer, well below the rank of the minister, and his job is to make extracts for the minister; a dispatch so short that it denies the officer the satisfaction of summarizing it will probably strengthen his scepticism about the ambassador.

The annual ambassadors' conference resolves this dilemma. Each ambassador brings with him a short paper analysing the situation in his post as it bears on the interests of his own country or as it affects the international alignment of forces. He can be questioned and criticized by his colleagues and made to amplify his statements, to draw out their implications at greater length or to produce more supporting evidence than the brevity of the paper will allow.

Furthermore, his colleagues play an important part in maturing the writer's understanding of his host country. They will add observations on the foreign policy of that state as expressed by its diplomats in their own postings. The writer, although the designated expert on the particular country at the conference, will receive from his brother ambassadors refinements of analysis, as indeed will the foreign ministry as a whole, the overall gains being shared by all. Each ambassador then goes back to his posting with greater knowledge and understanding. Each also goes back with some questions, the focus of which would have been considerably sharpened by the discussion. To return to one's post with a well-defined awareness of what a number of states are doing is to take back the confidence of clarity and range. As the ambassadors read the records of the discussion (and it is robbing the conference of its impact if only the resolutions are recorded), they will have a stronger grasp of the play of forces at the global level. Consequently, when ambassadors of another nation put forward proposals, they will, having first examined them to ensure they are precise, be able to respond decisively.

This is one of the less obvious boons an annual ambassadors' conference brings to the whole foreign service. Heads of mission do not incur the cost of frequent use of their telex machines to relay barrages of questions to headquarters. They will use telex only for an unexpected development, and even then they will be able to add helpful observations to their queries.

In diplomacy, as in the dance, a good performance calls for sureness of footing. Certainly this is one of the benefits an annual conference confers on its members. It provides them with an overall view of the whole foreign service and the relationships between the executive, the foreign ministry and the missions, as well as the importance of each in the total strategy, and thus it defines for each ambassador his function. The overview to which each ambassador is exposed at the conference is set within the global picture, with its points of strain, possible areas of collision and elements that are strong or weak or likely to collapse. Thus the ambassador is provided with a degree of forewarning. The conference does more. It gives him a fair estimate of the international forces working for accommodation, those working for confrontation and those working ambiguously.

He cannot operate effectively without these understandings, and to improve his comprehension, his country's United Nations representative should have a crucial role at the conference. Not only should that officer present his own paper on the disposal of forces in the UN itself, but he should also be active in each discussion on individual countries. Thus his own perceptions are sharpened by a knowledge of the bilateral behaviour of UN member-countries.

Also available to members of the conference should be the leading delegates to recent important international gatherings such as those on the law of the sea, world food, energy, population, information, human habitation and the United Nations Conference on Trade and Development. But supremely important for an ambassador's understanding of what is going on in the broad spectrum of the developing world are the reports by the delegates to various non-aligned conferences, whether at summit or committee level. Since South–South consultations have recently been emerging with encouraging frequency, the ambassadors in conference should be exposed to the experiences of those who attend them.

Ambassadors will, of course, have received copies of resolutions passed at such conferences as well as summaries of the discussions. But a written record of this type cannot deal with all the subtleties, the different concepts, the shifts in emphasis and in positions or the contradictions that eventually result in compromise. These can however be passed on at the ambassadors' conference either in formal sessions or in informal talks.

At the annual ambassadors' conference, cabinet ministers and senior bureaucrats can discuss local internal developments. It is better to do it as a joint exercise. Each ambassador can then see how each ministry fits in with the overall development thrust of the country. For his conceptual framework this is indispensable, and for his day-to-day relations with the host government it is crucial. An ambassador must not only know what each home ministry is doing, he must also know what are its major projects and plans for at least a year, and which of those projects and plans will need the technical cooperation of the government of the country to which he is posted. He can also advise the minister of a particular department whether any proposed project would strike a responsive chord with the government to which he is accredited and, if so, which agency or agencies should be approached.

There is a practical advantage to be gained from discussions with ministers and their mandarins that, again, no written communication can provide. It often happens that a ministry is seeking technical co-operation for the same project in two different countries with a view to obtaining the most favourable terms. This can lead, and often has, to a situation in which both countries are equally ready to assist. Negotiations continue with each to the final stage, when a choice is made. In such a case the two ambassadors concerned are in the dark about each other's instructions to proceed until, at the final moment, one of them is told to 'cool it'. This not only causes embarrassment to the ambassador who has to stop negotiations, it also engenders scepticism among aid agencies, who thus become much more critical in the scrutiny of projects presented to them by the country in question – and much more demanding.

There is a second reason for collective discussion between ambassadors and cabinet ministers and their mandarins. The end of empire began empire building among ministries in developing countries. It is not uncommon to find contradictions of policy between ministries, pursued with an energy and ingenuity disruptive to national goals. Some ministries conduct their own foreign policy, making their own arrangements with aid agencies and multinational corporations without even consulting the ministry of foreign affairs.

A dilemma is often posed in the relations between a developing country's ministry of foreign affairs and its other ministries (excepting the office of the head of government). If the ministry of foreign affairs regulates the external work of other ministries, it is seen as too powerful. But if it does not have some say in what its sister ministries do outside the country, then contradictions in the country's foreign policy will arise. Many of these contradictions are not at first seen for what they are. They proceed from the desire of the ministries to be effective and from an impatience with what they regard as the tortuous deliberations of the foreign ministry. They also arise from the understandable ambitions of ministers to enlarge their radius of action by securing the best technical and financial co-operation for development where they can find it.

In the resolution of these conflicts, ambassadors have an important role, which is best played collectively. They bring to the local situation perspectives gained from the detachment of distance. They are able to analyse the contradictory effects of ministerial actions on the societies to which they are posted. This is intimacy-at-a-distance. It renders the ambassadors as necessary to the maintenance of the conceptual framework of the country's development thrust as are the politicians, their advisers and theoreticians at home. In fact, heads of mission if they are permitted can greatly enlighten the home societies' understanding of themselves. They see their country from the outside in and the world from the inside out.

In particular, they are well placed to point out contradictions within the system that weaken the conceptual framework, stymie the development thrust and restore the dependency syndrome. In developing societies, such contradictions are particularly evident in dealings with foreign investment and transnational corporations; they can also arise from procedures, processes and even lifestyles. Ambassadors can not only quickly spot those contradictions (if they are not prime exponents of the contradictions themselves), but they can point out their effects. They are, of course, 'assisted' in this matter by those critics of Third-World countries who are always ready to highlight such inconsistencies as they can find.

All societies suffer from contradictions, and being aware of this is an important part of a Third-World ambassador's armoury. He will astutely admit to contradictions in his own society as a counterpart to those in the developed world. For instance, he can point out that there are countries whose total opposition to apartheid does not prevent their granting tax preferences to certain imports from South Africa. Canada is one. Again, he can point to the great power that categorically condemns communism but whose view of its self-interest allows diplomatic and economic relations with a communist giant. And he can remind his interlocutors of this conundrum: for some Western states, a Third-World country cannot be democratic enough – provided its government retains a conservative character. Doing this sort of thing and doing it well ('well' here meaning without getting into an adversary situation), he will lay the groundwork for intelligent dialogue and mutual respect between developed and developing societies. What he has to get across to his audiences in the rich countries is that every situation has its own inherent dialectic.

Ambassadors at their annual conference have, therefore, two blessings to confer on their societies: clarity and comparison. Through the blessing of clarity, unnecessary but unacknowledged contradictions are exposed and the stage is set for their resolution. Through the blessing of comparison, the society sees itself against other societies, even of more developed ones. It sees it does not have to become paranoid over its own imperfections; the fact that its evolution is dialectical is no reason for loss of confidence.

If Third-World ambassadors are to play these dual roles well, an annual fortification of their confidence and equipment is necessary. I am assuming, of course, that a Third-World ambassador is not viewed solely as an advocate whose duty is to obey his brief with mechanical competence. That view of him would rule out much discretionary action at his posting, and he would be unlikely to provide any useful critical assessment of his country's foreign policy.

Obedience practised with subtle and sensitive assessment is in any ambassador far more useful to his country than unquestioning compliance with instructions. The annual conference, as long as it is not an exercise in pedagogy, confirms this habit of mind and thus allows it to mature. This is the sort of ambassador that Third-World countries ought to send to the societies of the West, where the intellectual climate is one of criticism, debate, assessment and continuous review, at many levels and in many forums.

All this may be quite true. None the less, some small countries may not be able to afford an annual ambassadors' conference. But if to hold it annually is financially taxing, not to hold it at all or to hold it at capricious intervals is strategically and intellectually barren. As usual, there is a middle way – say a bi-annual conference composed not of all the ambassadors, but of representatives from different regions who can contribute insights from differing perspectives. Such an arrangement will not give all the detail a full conference does, but it will allow those present to review a broad range of the issues of the world of the 1980s.

If bi-annual conferences with a small, select attendance are the rule, then regular local conferences in regions that have clusters of missions should not be exceptions. They can be held in one of the region's capitals, one with good access and facilities where such a meeting will pose no awkward diplomatic problems. The discussions will naturally centre on the political, economic and diplomatic contours of the countries in the region – their relationships, actual or potential, with the home country and their individual and collective attitudes to the North–South dichotomy. It is important to hold these conferences after the bi-annual one at headquarters, so the ambassadors who attended it can report on its proceedings, giving the full background to the various issues.

Four aims should dominate these meetings: first, to see the region from the standpoint of the home country; second, to see the world from the standpoint of the region; third, to select up-to-date tactics relevant to the circumstances of each country for implementing the home country's strategies in the region; fourth, to exchange information on the region for the use of headquarters as well as of each ambassador. Finally, a comprehensive, well-documented report should follow each such meeting.

In all this, it is wise to remember the words of an eminent world statesman: 'If the Third World does not organize for the era of negotiations, even the fruits of victory already won at home will be yet lost.'[6] Ramphal was talking about structures for negotiation, but his words could apply to structures for thought, from which strategies for negotiation emerge. Some Third-World countries have made their foreign services not only instruments of high quality but organisms of coherent, analytical character. Other developing countries have yet to achieve this, and the disparity partially explains the difficulties of organizational and structural co-operation between the various states of the South.

Incidentally, the institution of annual or bi-annual ambassadors' conferences will save money in two ways: first, the reduced use of the telex or telephone to brief heads of mission; second, obviating the frequent need to summon ambassadors to headquarters for briefings – a sad reflection on the lack of intelligent economy in relations between the headquarters and missions of many a Third-World country. For instance, there will hardly be any need to send an ambassador a full-length telexed copy of a speech every time he has accepted the invitation to deliver one. Thanks to the insights gained at the conference, he will be able to compose it himself. Nor will he have to seek lengthy instructions every day from headquarters to allow him to get through his duties and cope with any unforeseen eventuality.

In short, his Ex will not live by Telex alone.

In one sense the Third-World ambassador is at the centre of things governmental, even though he is physically at a distance. But in another sense he is at the frontiers, watching for and analysing changes of mood or shifts of emphasis or new balances of power in the society of his posting. Signs of these changes can be detected in the political, economic or, frequently, academic spheres of the host country.

How? As I pointed out earlier, the daily trivia of an ambassador's life leave him with insufficient time for reading. But when the clink of glasses and the echoes of platitudes are silent, he still has to talk to officials who, themselves under no obligation to go to cocktails and dinners, are under every obligation to make their government's case watertight. Clearly the Third-World ambassador cannot read all the crucial books all the time, and he may not be able to read even some of the necessary books some of the time. But if he reads none of the important books at any time, he is not serving the interests of the developing world or that quarter of it that is his own country. He must not only be aware that there is a great deal of homework being done on either side of the poverty curtain, he must also have a grasp of what that homework is. It is at this point that the Third-World academic becomes important to the Third-World ambassador. Each ministry of foreign affairs should retain the services of a group of academics whose function – other than what they do at the university – is to bring to the ministry's attention important works in global economics and international affairs, whether published in the First, Second or Third Worlds. It is part of their routine academic business to review the publications of other academics as well as authors at the World Bank, the International Monetary Fund, the United Nations Educational, Scientific and Cultural Organization, the Club of Rome and other international bodies whose published works deal with issues of power, distribution, food, communications, energy and so on. But for Third-World academics to confine their analyses of these publications to learned journals only is to contain wisdom. Few of the harried senior foreign-service officers at home and fewer of the ambassadors abroad have the time or means to look up these critiques, especially if the jargon in which they are written makes reading them a simultaneous job of translation and comprehension.

There is a curious irony here. Third-World ambassadors in developed countries may have easy access to all the latest publications, even those published in their own part of the world, but little time to read them. The officers of the foreign ministry at home may have some time to read them but little access to them, except of course at the university library, where the competition for their use is very strong. The academics can play their part by preparing for ambassadors digests of the most useful publications, summarizing the main points, outlining the data on which conclusions are based as well as commenting on illogicalities or weaknesses. If the work is written from a Third-World point of view to substantiate the Third-World case, the role of the academic is all the more vital. By summarizing the main points and most telling arguments he or she can provide the ambassador with ammunition to support his representation in the country of his posting.

Make no mistake about it. Many Third-World ambassadors do buy the books produced by Third-World thinkers. But their daily routine and its daily interruptions permit them only to skip quickly through these works – hardly the best way for making good use of them. Sometimes they do have some time to read relevant material, but they do not always find that material readily, unless they can be directed where to look for it. Here again, academics are useful in preparing lists of works published or articles produced and places where they can be found.

There are times when distinguished writers from the Third World are called upon to distil their thinking in the form of speeches. These are useful to an ambassador because of their brevity; as lectures they will be lively and specific. For example there is a short course of lectures delivered by the distinguished Third-World economist, Mahbub Ul Haq, at the University of Guyana in 1974. Those lectures were a skilful, sensitive and elegant digest of his major work, *The Poverty Curtain.*[7] They were subsequently turned into a small booklet under the Turkeyn lecture series and are useful not only to ambassadors and Third-World diplomats, but to those in developed countries who seek precisely this kind of distillation.

Academics are congenitally given to tracking things down for themselves and their students. It is a wise foreign minister that taps this passion for bibliography. One of the definitions of diplomacy is the manipulation of the immediate in the interests of the ultimate. For the proper practice of this manipulation, an ambassador from the Third World needs both an overview (the broad picture) and an underview (the details).

Objectives call for strategies to achieve them, and strategies call for various tactics for the various situations. The temptation of an ambassador in his frenzied rush is to take care of the tactics and let the strategies take care of themselves. But he cannot afford to do that, nor can the globe afford to have him do it, for human survival and civilization as we know it are at stake in the last two decades of the twentieth century. The Third-World ambassador exists to prove that a global community is possible and that diplomats can help create the vision that will lead to it.

4 The Alternative Lexicon: Diplomats and the Media

That sinister exponent of mind control, Josef Stalin, used to say that of all the monopolies enjoyed by the Soviet state, none was so crucial as its monopoly over the definition of words. The ultimate weapon of political control was the dictionary.

Television was not then the powerful medium it is now, so he did not refer to it. But his dictum applies to the screen as to other media. It involves the selection of some words and phrases as symbols of self-evident truths and rejection of others as symbols of self-evident falsehoods. Even more potent, because more subtle, is the tacit ignoring of those words and phrases that imply a questioning of settled conviction.

This strategy of selection, rejection and overlooking is found in capitalist as well as communist societies. For every society has an ideology. Some societies proclaim it in nearly every circumstance and through all official voices; others assume rather than assert it. In a few it is so pervasive that members of the society uncon- sciously subscribe to it. Ideology, they assure themselves, is the systematic self-deception with which the gods have afflicted their adversaries.

People see on the screen, hear on the radio or read in the papers fundamentally what supports the prevailing doctrine. Criticisms of these doctrines are occasionally allowed. Occa- sionally, however, is the operative word; the media aim at consensus of prevailing norms. Thus, while Western democracies allow nearly every point of view free expression, what that freedom means in practice is the right of the proponents to finance their own media to give their convictions utterance.

This situation is important to the Third World, because it stands for a new lexicon – one of perceptions not of wealth, but of poverty, not of support for the international *status quo*, but of the need for change. It is difficult for Third-World ambassadors to present their alternative lexicon in the face of the established power of the media in the societies of their posting – and the fears, phobias or sheer contempt for the developing world that those media networks tend to foment.

Third-World ambassadors in developed countries face therefore the problem of making their convictions acceptable. This problem is deepened by the fact that the part of the world they represent does not have reliable access to the media of Western nations.

On the other hand, as explained briefly earlier in this book, it hears about itself as the rich nations talk about it. Much of the material broadcast and published in the media of the developing nations originates with Western-controlled agencies – news agencies, features syndicates and the resale departments of TV and radio networks.

Typically what happens is that, in any one developing country, local newspapers and broadcasting stations will report developments within that country. But they tend to take reports about other developing countries from the agency networks or the syndicates. And these are Western-controlled.

The present international information order asks the Third World to see itself through the eyes of the First – which means in effect that the Third World is invited to believe that its backwardness and misery are the result of its own deficiencies. Such a conviction, if it hardens, would not lead to any demand for a change of the present world system because the system would not then be seen as the cause of the problem. It would lead to an acceptance of infinitesimal gains as being the only form of progress available to developing societies while the gap between them and the rich countries continues to widen. It is this state of affairs that is at the bottom of the developing world's demand for a new international information order (NIIO). Let the Third World write about the Third World.

As long as the Third World hears about itself from the First, then what is being asked for is its accommodation to the *status quo*: an acceptance of poverty as a self-generating condition, however galling it may be to admit it. This is what is actually happening with the present international information order. It is axiomatic that if you control the images that people see and the words that they hear or read, you control their perceptions of reality.

Thus, it is intended that the prevailing order be acquiesced in by those to whom it gives most pain.

The first task of a Third-World ambassador to a developed society is therefore to put compellingly to the barons of the media and their clients the need to reverse their opposition toward the NIIO. It should be remembered that this proposed order is seen by most media specialists in the rich countries either as an impediment to the free flow of information or a denial of the basic human right to take information from wherever it comes and pass it on to wherever it is supposed to be needed. Some media pundits even claim that the demand for the NIIO represents a reluctance to allow Third-World people open access to information their governments do not control or cannot doctor.

Underlying this opposition is an assumption that news from developed countries is free from ideological bias, an 'objective' reporting of facts as they are. The assumption is false, and the ambassador and his staff will naturally counter it.

No news reporting can be wholly free from bias. Some ideological underpinning to words and images used by any society is inevitable. News is a combination of facts and perception, the facts falling into place as support for perceptions, with emphasis ensuring the required emotional resonances. Perceptions vary with history, locality, vital interests of opposing kinds, power (or lack of it), wellbeing (or the need for it) and, above all, consciousness. It is chimerical to expect that the initial reaction to news in one context will be the same as in another.

For example, the initial reaction of the people of Britain to the 1973 oil-price hike was not the same as that of the people of OPEC (Organization of Petroleum Exporting Countries); nor, more significantly, were the reactions of the Japanese and the Americans the same. Few Americans (within and without the Reagan administration) view the El Salvador situation as do Western Europeans. In each case a perception of danger or the possibility of discomfort initially shaped the reactions from which the interpretation of events was hewn.

I mentioned above that consciousness contributes to a people's perceptions. During the long colonial sleep, the circles of certainty for the peoples of the Third World lay in the imperial capitals. Accordingly, even though their initial reactions to events may have differed from those of their colonial overlords, they eventually fell into line. Independence has brought to most

Third-World countries a greater sense of self. The circles of certainty are increasingly located for these nations not in the rich Western countries, nor in the Communist ones, but in their own. No longer when they look at events do they evaluate their significance from a First-World position; they know they do not belong to that order. The points of reference are different. Affluence sustains a concept of the world that necessarily contradicts the one sustained by poverty.

The central conviction for Third-World peoples is that their survival is in question. All other conclusions spring from that. It is therefore no longer axiomatic for them that whatever is good for the rich is good for themselves. They will refuse to accept news from developed countries based on such an axiom, and this refusal has been shaped by that most severe of schools, experience.

Third-World ambassadors will find in rich societies indications that borrowing perceptions from the powerful is not considered legitimate by the less powerful. For instance, Canada and the United States are the world's greatest trading partners, and their defence systems are closely linked. But Canadians reject any notion that their country is an Arctic extension of the US. They insist that Canada is a middle power, neither a satellite nor a subsidiary of Washington. Their perceptions, they argue, on vital internal or international matters are bound to be different from those of a superpower (especially one with a penchant for feeling itself threatened every time a small ally shows signs of determining its domestic arrangements by its own criteria). Not only do Canadians defend their right not to take their understanding of the world from Washington, they also argue that it is flying in the face of nature to expect them to see things in exactly the same way as their neighbour.

Yet they are both capitalist societies, members of the Western alliance, and they both claim an immunity (albeit a fallacious one) from ideologic fervour. The Parliament of Canada has ensured that Canadians see themselves in their own mirrors. They have the publicly owned Canadian Broadcasting Corporation, and legislation has ensured it is virtually impossible for private radio and television or any publications to be operated by non-Canadians. What is true of Canada is true of Britain, which has a publicly owned broadcasting system and a controlled-ownership private broadcasting system. British newspapers show a truculent disregard for any attempts by outside interests to influence their views. The same goes for every other country in Western Europe. To be sure, the media in some of these countries take news from the large press agencies and syndicates, but only about nations of which they know nothing or little. They do not take news about themselves from anywhere other than from among themselves. On their own situations they are the final authorities, whatever the Associated Press, Canadian Press or Press Association may say (and let us remember that these organizations are news co-operatives, controlled by the subscribing newspapers).

In short, the media of the West will not allow foreigners, however gargantuan their networks or Olympian their reportage, to decide for them what is important about themselves.

The nations just referred to are comfortable and rich. They do not need an NIIO, because the old order serves them well. The Third-World ambassador has to explain this in putting the case for the NIIO. He will show that even under similar conditions of wealth, shared orthodoxy and comfort, different peoples develop different perceptions.

But the vast majority of Third-World peoples do not live under such conditions. For many of them the *status quo* is equivalent to their own extinction, and change must come. It will come largely by the pressure they put on the present system and the way they organize themselves to mount that pressure. Organization means rigorous, continuous thought, which is impossible to minds saturated with images and ideas beamed by the developed world media.

The Third-World ambassador has a duty to point out the relationship between perception and motivation, as it applies to nations. People who read of themselves only as victims of disaster, disorder or disease (physical or political) can hardly think of themselves as creators of wealth or opportunity. The fatalism for which they are often condemned is frequently the product of the fatalism by which they are often reported.

There seem to be two magnets of fascination for the media of developed societies: eccentric success and numbing disaster. The media ignore achievement, which is not the same thing as success. Achievement implies not the winning of a race, but patient endurance of difficulties, the falling to rise again, the learning as you go, an all-round lifting of levels rather than a singular and spectacular exploit.

To report not the achievements, but only the successes of a people is to report the favoured few, not the attempting many, and then to dismiss the latter as nonstarters. For success is invariably seen as measuring up to the standards the West has achieved, and few developing countries can do that given the constraints the West has imposed on them. Western journalists as a whole concentrate on what they describe as the failures of Third-World countries, on the natural or economic disasters from which they suffer and particularly on the foibles of some of their political leaders.

But there are achievements, wrested from hostile circumstances, worthy of being reported – the gradual raising of some developing countries to self-sufficiency in crucial areas, the adaptive and often creative use of scarce resources, the recycling of used components of technology, the intelligent search for alternative sources of energy, a revolution in dietary habits. These seldom see print in those journals that purport to cover developments in the Third World, journals that find a barren pleasure in highlighting the bizarre coronation of a Bokassa, or the murderous antics of an Amin. Indeed the tragicomic makes good copy, but it seems nothing is less readable than real gains.

If the motto of much journalism is that bad news is good news and good news is no news, this is the strongest case for the NIIO. Without it, bad news in the developing world will never be seen in its proper perspective, and good news will hardly be seen or heard at all.

A Third-World ambassador who wants to point out how a people's morale is affected by the news and the way they receive it does not have to look far for an example that will command the respect of most in the West.

During 1940–1, Britain stood alone against the Axis powers, and the record of her humiliations was lengthy. But Winston Churchill had never ceased to be a journalist, whatever else he became. He sensed the relationship between news and interpretation on the one hand, perception and motivation on the other. He took words like 'withdrawal', 'retreat', 'surrender', 'capitulation' and 'defeat', and he turned them into emotional diminutives. Being a master of the alternative lexicon, he did not deny the bitter truths, but he redefined the possibilities and in doing so enlarged them. Many years later, President John Kennedy, commenting that Churchill had mobilized the English language and sent it into battle, put his finger on the vital element in that war leader's genius – the ability to marshall images that depicted resilience, defiance, confidence and victory.

The Third-World ambassador will clinch his point by reminding his hearers that Churchill possessed a potent weapon, the radio, to take his words not only into the homes and pubs of his countrymen, but around the world. The man had the medium to make his message universal.

Using analogies like these (he should ring the changes according to where he is), the ambassador can strengthen the case that Third-World peoples should have their own media networks to relay to the whole of the developing world the achievements of its parts. These networks would turn solid but unspectacular gains into lively reporting or measure a breakthrough by the weight of the factors stacked against it, and so help create a mood in which expectations are not influenced by rich societies. Most important of all, such networks will report pluses and minuses without weighting the latter. They will tell their audiences more about ploughboys than playboys and, because in this kind of journalism foreigners do not call the shots, there will be less talk of gunplay.

But the Third-World ambassador, in his relations with the local media, must do more than make the case for the NIIO. In a society that portrays poverty as an ethnic defect, it is the responsibility of himself and his staff to introduce the alternative lexicon and make its perceptions readily available to the media.

No easy task this, a far cry from the boozed comity of the cocktail circuit and the genial tentativeness of representational dinners. Journalists are usually tough, with strong persuasions. They are sceptical of the diplomats whose hospitality they both enjoy and distrust; ironically, they expect a standard of public probity in the Third World that would, if it existed in their own societies, rob them of most of their lead stories.

But not many of them have closed minds. A large number are humanists, as intolerant of unnecessary suffering as they are of unnecessary ineptitude. They are fascinated with novelty, either in concepts, fashions, structures or happenings, open to propositions of enlightened self-interest and concerned with the potent use of words and images.

A Third-World ambassador has to establish relations with the media that are more than purely defensive. This means that he must set out to acquire a working and comprehensive knowledge of the media establishment in the country of his posting – an establishment that, for his purposes, is as crucial and sometimes as powerful as that of the government to which he is accredited. It is, of course, a very different kind of establishment, moving to a very different drumbeat. It shares one of the great objectives of the political establishment – power. But it employs widely different methods for attaining it.

Where politicians and bureaucrats practise discretion, the media practise disclosure. Where the bureaucrats move by rumination and the politicians by alternate decision and delay, the media move by airwaves and laser beams. The political establishment seeks to regulate society's behaviour by structuring it; the media seek to shape people's minds by image and impact. Both have a virile sense of indispensability and sometimes even vie for supremacy. The conventional wisdom had it that the politicians make the news and the media report it; the reality is that *both* make the news.

Of the working journalists with whom he is likely to come into contact (this excludes editors, owners and usually such types as sports journalists and other peripheral specialists), the Third-World ambassador can conveniently think of five categories:

- The hard-news journalist. These tend to pigeon-hole the world into sweeping universals and report everything as encapsulations of one or other of them.
- The human-interest specialist. These delight in illustrating the endearing or endangering eccentricities of their fellow-people.
- Investigative journalists. These subscribe apparently to the conspiracy theory of history and see their duty as being to expose these conspiracies.
- Humanists. These are passionately concerned with man's inhumanity to man and use the power of the media to restrain it.
- Educationalists. These see the media as instruments of enlightenment and themselves as teachers.

There is, of course, some overlapping in these categories. For instance a hard-news journalist may decide to investigate corruption or an investigative type may investigate inhumanity in local prisons. But the ambassador will learn to distinguish which type of work each of his journalistic friends leans toward.

Of these categories, the group he is obviously likely to have the least fruitful contact with is the second, inasmuch as they are not concerned with the flexibility of systems but the caprice of individuals. In some countries the third group embraces practitioners who are against governments in general and Third-World governments in particular. Others of this group seek Marxist conspiracies, with which they confuse every attempt to replace privilege with justice or to help the poor.

Groups one, four and five are likely to welcome contacts with ambassadors from the developing world. But within these groups are conservatives and non-conservatives, whom ambassadors with sensitive antennae will quickly detect. For instance, a sizeable number of group one, concerned though they are with broad, sweeping movements of perception, prescription and action, are robust First Worlders more ready to sell the universals of the West than to integrate them into more transcending universals.

Again, not all those concerned with man's inhumanity to man recognize the cruelty of structural imbalance. Some are more concerned with obvious acts of political tyranny, ethnic intolerance, religious bigotry, terrorism and the suppression of the rights of the individual. Wise ambassadors will not eschew these more conservative types, but they will recognize that converting and broadening their present beliefs will be a process demanding patience.

Communications with the more liberal members of groups one, four and five can be very constructive if ambassadors bring to the dialogue not just an understanding of the preoccupations of journalists, but also that expertise on international issues mentioned in Chapter 3. For instance, central to the liberal ethic are human rights – particularly equality of opportunity and freedom to choose between political creeds. Third-World thinkers concern themselves with other, equally fundamental rights: the right to stay alive, the right to food and nutrition, the right to unpolluted water and to a decent domicile and the right to work. The Western liberal sees the human condition as one of freedom or the lack of it; those of the Third World see the human condition in terms of deprivation or the removal of it. Each side has taken a great truth and from it drawn incomplete conclusions.

The representatives of the developing world can establish with media figures the connection between these two fundamentals. For instance, the sturdiness of choice in any situation presupposes a minimum of nutrition. Equality of opportunity is only meaning-ful when people are free from the imperatives of survival to grasp those opportunities. In short, malnutrition and disease do not make good soil for dissent or ascent.

How then should the Third-World ambassadors and their staffs present the alternative vision?

The starting point is a people's collective experience, the history that is bred deep in its bones. For Western societies, their past is at once their heritage, the testament for their identity, their justification and the mirror of their collective consciousness.

The countries of Western Europe, Canada, Australia and New Zealand all have their preferred though undogmatic national destinations – destinations not as clamantly orchestrated as those of the two superpowers, each of whose declared destiny is to put the other out of commission. With some of those countries the aim is national security by non-bellicose means; with others it is consensus by reducing class conflict and creating political and economic structures that lead to national vibrancy. There are those that work at making competitiveness the high road to excellence while minimizing class conflict. One or two of them see in their culture and their language instruments for regenerating civilization's flagging energies. But all of them have this in common: they want economic buoyancy, internal and interna-tional peace and personal comfort.

In the contemplation of the future, they look instinctively back, although they do not think of themselves as backward-looking. History for them is a kind of moral bank. It is for most Europeans and North Americans not only hindsight but insight. Former skills, strengths, aptitudes and capabilities are not regarded as lost; they are a potent latency. The collective psyche is a tremendous storehouse, and different crises evoke responses that are a complex of experiences drawn from many past challenges. This bank and its deposits must be a subject for thorough study by Third-World ambassadors. They can draw on it in presenting their case.

For instance, a Third-World ambassador can agree with those who say Marx wrongly predicted the working classes in the West would overthrow the system because of their deepening depriva-tion. He can also agree why it was that Marx was wrong – had the expectations of the industrial poor grown much faster than the improvement in their conditions, Marxist projections would have had a revolutionary confirmation. But patricians and the bourgeoisie sensed the hint of revolution. As the poor organized to improve their lot or bring down their 'betters', the latter extended the political and economic benefits of the system. They thus enabled change to take place with stability and stability to be compatible with change. The increasing political organization of the poor was matched by the increasing political flexibility of the rich.

Even Bismarck, that astute instinctual conservative, gave industrial security to the Germany of his day by giving personal security to the wage earners. He based the German imperial system not only on the celebrated blood and iron (or the less-celebrated coal and iron), but on social security and old-age pensions for workers. Bismarck, a Third-World voice can point out, understood on a national level a century ago what many of his successors, the neo conservatives, do not understand on a global level today: that the body politic in which the rich make no allowances for the hopes of the poor stagnates. Or worse, it exists in a state of anxiety. A Third-World diplomat with a sense of history will have many examples from which to choose.

In his dialogue with the media, a Third-World diplomat should point to the two stages by which the position of the poor in capitalist societies came to be remedied. The first was the discovery that the poor were organizing to protect themselves from the rapacity of employers and the connivance of the state. In this it can be demonstrated that the poor were frequently helped by some members of the upper classes with conscience to recognize injustice or prescience to recognize danger. (The parallel is with those in Western countries who today are trying to explain to businessmen, policymakers and thoughtful fellow-citizens the immorality and inexpediency of the present lopsided world system.) Next was that, as the organizations of the poor began to acquire toughness and astuteness, the rich had to decide between confrontation and accommodation.

In those societies that adopted the more realistic policy of accommodation, the transition from exclusive to shared power was seldom revolutionary. Those societies showed a remarkable resilience and continuity, even under the test of war; if anything they came out of war more broadly based than they had gone into it. They were not subject to the disruptions or social upheavals of those societies that kept economic and political power at the top.

The Third-World ambassador can point to this experience of the peoples of Western Europe, North America, Australia and New Zealand. It should, he will assert, now be applied on a global level. During the past two centuries, the now-developed nations have seen their futures more as the motor of the present than as a continued but slightly modified version of their pasts. Thus, for Western people, the past is experience and the future is stimulus. Neither should suggest they be complacent about the present.

Another line of argument from the experience of rich nations is their ability to make customers out of the poor. That was the basis of the thinking of John Maynard Keynes and of the New Deal of Franklin Delano Roosevelt. It is one of the bases of the consumer ethic. The poor are no use to an economy, except to give it sweated labour, and this the rise of trade unionism has largely precluded.

But the poor are of great use to an economy as purchasers. They stimulate the expansion of wealth, to their own satisfaction while spending it, albeit this does not seriously deprive those who are accumulating the wealth. What the poor earn they spend. Thus instead of being marginal purchasers, the large mass of people become substantial ones. It is the opposite of the theory, seriously held by some, that the poverty of the poor is the guarantee of the wealth of the rich. The ambassador will make it clear that wealth besieged leads finally to the erosion of the comfort of the wealthy, whereas unbesieged wealth is more secure because those who have it are included among the many who share.

When an ambassador can persuade his interlocutors that the social security of wealth and its immunity from recession or depression lie in the inclusion of the poor, he will have created a watershed in the thinking of the rich. But he must lead this argument from within the experience of rich societies. Only then can he convincingly dwell on the vast millions on the global scene yearning to be fed, but still living below subsistence level, who cannot be customers of the rich societies unless their condition is changed from a struggle for survival to one of taking part in productive life. He will also remind his media friends that the combined populations of the rich countries are a diminishing fraction of the earth's total. Arithmetic alone ought to impel the rich to conclude that their self-interest lies in enabling the developing world to do business with them.

The diplomat can illustrate his point by the economic per-plexities of the developed countries, whether communist or capitalist. The importance to them of the Third World was demonstrated in 1974 and 1975, when recession was averted largely by the modest revenues flowing from developing societies. These revenues derived from the minimal purchases the develop-ing nations were able to make plus interest and dividends they paid on loans and investments.

Media practitioners like to quote Marshall McLuhan's 'global village'. But more often than not, they mean by this a village of global communications not a village of mutual obligations. The Third-World diplomat can agree that we are intermeshed as never before, but our enmeshment is productive not of increasing stability, but of an increasing acrimony that is leading to explosiveness in one area after another of the developing world.

He can easily demonstrate that the village is rapidly becoming a series of fortresses in which the heightening hostility of the two most redoubtable ones – the United States and the Soviet Union – forces ever more fanatic competition for support from the weaker ones. The vulnerability or volatility of the weak thus determines the behaviour of the strong; the Third World's tinderbox poverty or growing exasperation is becoming the regulator of peace (or lack of it) for the international community as a whole.

Nor will he have to labour the point to knowledgeable journalists that the Second Cold War is practically on its way. And a far less optimistic Third World than existed during the first Cold War may be crucial to the temperature of that conflict. If he reads anything from the Vatican (and he should) he will be able to quote Pope Paul VI's far-sighted dictum, 'The new name for peace is development.'[8]

The argument for continuing the historical experience of prosperity, comfort and security for the rich is much more likely to gain attention and recognition among media buffs than is the artillery of moral outrage. Ethical arguments may be presented as the crystallization of Western social experience. Thus, before 1945 in many European countries, the poor were pitied, but abolishing poverty was considered utopian; after 1945 the organization of society rendered poverty not only a diminishing problem but almost an unnatural one. In fifty years there had been a social revolution. Ethics had been the handmaiden of expediency. Those who could hardly tolerate poverty in their midst were only two generations away from those who could hardly imagine Europe without the poor.

It is not the business of Third-World ambassadors to provide the media with publishable opportunities for irony. It *is* their business to make convergence – or, better, consensus – not merely convincing as a front but palpable as a policy. They should present their consensus not as conspiracy, but as a necessity in the best interests of humanity, based on the same principles, globally applied, as those of the North Atlantic Treaty Organization, the European Economic Community, the Warsaw Pact and even that less formal arrangement of co-operative antagonism known as *détente*.

For ambassadors to get to know journalists is nowadays a *sine qua non* of their profession. It is now equally imperative that groups of Third-World ambassadors, especially those with common strategies of development, should work out common approaches to the media to produce an overall consistency. Heads of missions should meet regularly to agree on media guidelines so that they individually take the same line of reasoning that they do when they act collectively.

Pooling what they know about the media and its personalities is a priority. Having identified media people interested in development issues – even those less receptive than prescriptive – they should then arrange regular meetings with them. Lunches or dinners provide time to talk and answer questions, and each ambassador can offer his country's experience as an aspect of the case or an example. Senior media personnel are busy people. They would find it more convenient to attend collective sessions with ambassadors than to accept many individual invitations. Most diplomats too are busy and cannot meet each sympathetic journalist regularly. That is why collective lunches or dinners serve both sides equally well. Before such sessions ambassadors with differing skills arising out of diverse backgrounds will decide among themselves who will do what. For instance, one will be adroit enough to handle the questions on trade, another will handle debt servicing, another the law of the sea, one commodity stabilization and one the implications of import substitution. The important thing is to have each ambassador able to speak comprehensively in an interlocking presentation.

These sessions amount to teach-ins on development in which the professors are everyday practitioners with a working knowledge of both the details and the broad perspective of their subject. The stimulus of these meetings is change – either fear of it, the need for it, the pressure of it or the understanding of it. The objective is perception. The difficulties that arise in these meetings are often due to the preconceptions of those who attend. To grapple with such preconceptions is the *raison d'être* of such activity.

Journalists are people in a hurry. They read hungrily, but their reading is subject to certain imperatives: there are items they must study or they will have no job, items they must ponder or they will have no sweep, and finally items at which they merely glance because they have no time. The concerns of developing countries are often in the last category. Journalists have some knowledge of what developing countries want but little under-standing of what, within their limits, they are doing or exactly why their demands for a change in the world system are so insistent. Regular sessions between groups of Third-World ambassadors and leading media people can deepen the latter's knowledge and, more important, their awareness, without imposing on them the Herculean labour of all the reading necessary to reach a full awareness.

Some of the more scholarly-minded will want to be guided to material that provides more information than do the recommen-dations and resolutions of international conferences. Having an idea of the position taken by developing countries, they want to know how that position crystallized. There are carefully docu-mented, rigorously researched and thoughtfully articulated works of experts, written from within the Third-World experience, that also reveal awareness of the concerns and conceptual norms of developed societies. Getting leading journalists of any developed society to follow the Third-World case from the pages of its most distinguished thinkers will itself be an achievement. For, in their dealings with the problems of development, the media of the First World often concentrate on irritation, on the polemics of podium presentations, rather than on the sobrieties of patient scholarship.

Underlying all this should be one central theme: the poor of this world are not to be held accountable for their poverty. However subtly, genially or wittily the ambassador expresses it, he should leave his listeners in no doubt as to its centrality.

If that is the point and purpose of an ambassador's message, how does he get it across to the media of the country of his posting?

The first principle is to acknowledge this: the less he does

singly, the more effective his witness will be. Granted, diplomacy
has by tradition and in practice been a competitive enterprise;
diplomats are bred and blooded to competition. But for the
Third-World ambassador in the 1980s, these practices bear no
relationship, as S. S. Ramphal, Commonwealth secretary-
general, puts it, 'to the needs to be served or the service to be
rendered'.[9] Competition among diplomats from the developing
world is grist for the mill of the media; divisions among the
proclaimed united make better copy than war among the known
divided. All the world loves a contradiction. Many a journalist
can sound profound by writing about 'the superb irony of the
situation', when he or she is being no more than obvious.

Not all speeches are devoid of mature thought, careful investi-
gation and creative insight. Consider, for instance, the collection
of speeches by Ramphal, *A World to Share*. This is a model for a
journalist seeking an advocacy of the Third World's case that
transcends the Third World. It will please journalists for another
reason. If their ideal is to communicate in passion that is
contagious, arguments that are logical and language that is
memorable, Ramphal's speeches are an exemplary of that ideal.

When media pundits become aware of the Third World's case,
the ambassadors will have made another breakthrough. They will
have taught the journalists that diplomats are not just merchants
of some temporary dogma. They are spokesmen for an alternative
world order that seeks to save the many who are poor yet not
destroy the few who are rich.

Heads of mission can find opportunities in important events
that take place in the Third World or between representatives of
the Third and First Worlds. They can explain to journalists the
nature and meaning of those events for the world as a whole. For
instance, there might be a meeting of the foreign ministers of
non-aligned countries. In each of the capitals of the developed
world groups of ambassadors from non-aligned states should host
a lunch or dinner for the people of the media. They should not
wait for a summit of the Non-Aligned Movement before mount-
ing such structured dialogues.

This is a germane point, because many First-World journalists
seem less concerned with the significance of such summits than
with the difficulties so varied an assemblage has in arriving at a
consensus. By way of a damage-limitations exercise Third-World
ambassadors can point out that the United States and Europe,

though strongly united ideologically and in defence, have considerable disagreements that demand patient negotiation and continuous reassessment.

Indeed representatives of the developing world have to spend much time pointing out the obvious: that the achievements of the Non-Aligned Movement should be seen in their proper context. Predictably, there are different emphases and ideologies among individual member states. To emphasize the problems of convergence rather than the achievement of consensus is an exercise in platitude. That can largely be obviated. Non-aligned ambassadors acting together can continuously expose First-World journalists to all facets of the movement. They can show how it has introduced new concepts of international accountability, even among developed nations. Such an exposure will be salutory for the journalist, challenging for the ambassadors and cementing for both sides.

Likewise, any of the great events of the Commonwealth, like the bi-annual heads of government meeting or even one of its periodic conferences of professionals, presents high commissioners with an opportunity. They can demonstrate to journalists how the Commonwealth works, what resources it uses, how it uses its pool of skills and what its contributions are to the whole concept of international co-operation. For here again there is often a large lag in understanding between what the Commonwealth is actually achieving and what journalists perceive it to be doing. This is especially so of those who don't read its publications or haven't personally seen it at work. This sort of situation gives the representatives of Commonwealth countries a scandalously large opportunity to demonstrate how often reality is far ahead of the media's conception.

Not all journalists – even the most sapient in member countries – yet see the Commonwealth as 'a slice of the world at the service of the world'.[10] The Commonwealth is not easy to define; it has no settled constitution, nor are its principles proclaimed by an identifiable manifesto. Accordingly it is often written off as an emotional attachment to the past or final proof of British conmanship in getting radically different people to ritualize their colonial subjugation. Some write about the Commonwealth as heterogeneity linked by language (true), a medium for superficial agreements that have no meaning for global cleavages (false).

What is so often missed by the media is the work of the Commonwealth and similar groupings: the intense cross-pollination of techniques, of experiences and experiments and of shared failures and successes. High commissioners and ambassadors of non-Commonwealth countries can be useful here, but the strategies they use are as important as the information they communicate. Remembering that the concrete is always more telling than the abstract, they should concentrate on the specifics of Commonwealth co-operation. Journalists like to say they live by facts. Too hard-boiled to be impressed by talk, they want to see what the Commonwealth does. To show them is the job of Commonwealth diplomats. They should flesh out their talk about Commonwealth mutuality by pointing to examples of it in their own countries and then placing those examples in the overall context of development. Abstraction is the enemy of good copy; action explained is its great ally.

The way Commonwealth projects are funded is as important as what is done with the funds. In any one project, more than one country may take part, and the expertise may come from a number of countries, developed and developing. This, done with exemplary economy, is an object lesson to journalists sceptical of, or positively opposed to, multilateral assistance and third country participation. Explaining this approach gives Commonwealth envoys a great opportunity to underline the demonstration effect of the Commonwealth, the fact that despite differences in wealth, culture and power, a healthy relationship between developed and developing countries is beginning. Thus is visible a pattern that, strengthened, will apply to larger-scale relationships. Conflict is not absent in the Commonwealth, the envoys will note. But conflict is balanced with accommodation. Seeking convergence to offset divergence is a philosophy more than just a method. It assumes the whole is greater than the self-interested sum of its parts.

When journalists and Third-World ambassadors meet frequently to talk about the world, confidence must ensue. The image of an ambassador as a conduit for telegraphed clichés will give way to that of an interpreter of alternative proposals for survival. Confidence of this sort is a gain for the international community as a whole. Its local effects in any one of the rich societies is likely to go beyond just a greater journalistic sensitivity to the issues of international reconstruction. For instance, Third-World ambassadors may be asked to assist or advise with radio or television documentaries on international affairs. Rather than shying away from this task, they should give it their cerebral best. It is more important to assist in the shaping of a series of programmes than to appear on one news item. Influencing the orientation of the series counts for more than the satisfaction the ambassador gets from reporting to his foreign minister that he has discussed his country's position in the media.

Not many ambassadors currently make a good showing on television, the most popular medium in North America and Europe, and to make a less-than-good showing is worse than to make no showing at all. Diplomats who are impressive on television should not neglect opportunities of appearing. But the high profile one has on television and the influence one has on those who shape its thrust are not the same thing. The Third-World ambassador cannot afford *not* to assist in shaping the pictures of his world that go out to millions of viewers in the affluent societies. As long as the opportunity is available (and the above suggest it can be created), he must use it.

If an ambassador's rapport with the leading media people is good, then whenever there is an item of news about his country, whether eye-catching, illustrative or disturbing, he will be consulted about it. This is the test of a diplomat's credibility in the country of his posting. He may be asked questions in a joint interview with others of opposite views. If he knows how to handle such a situation and does not go in for typically diplomatic evasions, he will be credible not only among the media practitioners, but among the public. If it is the sort of issue on which the wisest course is no comment, he has no business appearing on the media. If there is confidence between himself and the media pundits, they will respect his freedom of decision.

Far more effective than appearances on radio and television is the ambassador's influence on how the implications of the event are reported. News has been defined as, among other things, the art of emphasis. That definition could also apply to an ambassador's function. Thus, there is common ground between the two professions of diplomacy and journalism. This is convenient, inasmuch as the ambassador seeks the sort of media emphasis that is a window into the nature of the problem rather than a pulpit from which to deliver hasty judgements. This is a subtle, delicate exercise. Developing nations should post to the seminal capitals of the developed world diplomats with expertise in media affairs. They should be imbued with the delicacy necessary to relate to media practitioners and the camaraderie needed to develop those relationships.

Diplomatic missions, a cynic would say, exist primarily to publish handouts. Indeed, the practice of diplomacy today is almost inconceivable without those self-justifying bulletins. They range from the stark, cyclostyled records of presidential reflections to glossy, illustrated productions that smack of opulence and assurance. Ink and money are lavished on these publications, which fall like rain from the diplomatic heavens. But in the modern world's plenitude of clamorous paper there is little relationship between the energy that produces them and the attention they get. Most of them are destined for receptacles quite incompatible with their lofty origins.

The truth is: there are too many of them. Most have a catch-as-catch-can policy toward their potential readership. Some are so unattractive as to look like government gazettes. Others are so lush as to look like advertisements for trendy goods. Too often they are written at the top of their voices, either in self-righteous congratulation or sulphurous condemnation, the former being too blatant and the latter being too bellicose to sit comfortably with a good digestion. Few self-respecting journalists bother to read them, and fewer research fellows or university students take them seriously. The bureaucrats to whom they are copiously sent don't even bother to pass them on to their most junior officials. The energy that goes into turning them out could be more fruitfully used. Yet their production in the name of information is demanded by the governments at home; often special attachés are paid to keep up the flow.

Countries with scarce resources could just as well keep the money spent on them at home, as they are too obviously propagandist for most recipients to treat them positively.

All governments have found themselves virtually compelled to produce great quantities of information. Certainly nations are correct in placing so much emphasis on a commodity that can have an important impact on opinion outside their own borders. But that calls for imaginative strategy, not just to keep up with the publications of other missions. The aim is not competitiveness, especially with other developing countries, but effective use of the means available in regard to the readership projected. Strict criteria, therefore, should be applied to these publications to ensure that they are worth the resources put into them.

While a diplomatic publication is still at the planning stage, the first question to be settled is to whom it is addressed. No intelligently conceived newspaper, journal or magazine is launched without a specifically defined range of readers in mind. The publications of missions are intended for two groups of readers. First, the *cognoscente* – those who know something of the complexities of international affairs. Next, the intelligentsia – those without inside information who none the less seek to interpret and understand the forces, ideological or material, that are shaping their environment.

A Third-World mission has to decide whether the cause of development is better served by writing for the former or the latter. The *cognoscente* include the ministers, mandarins and bureaucrats of government departments, notably foreign affairs, and quasigovernment organizations, as well as members of parliament. To write for these means usually to write in the jargon of the trade to which they are accustomed. But these people have little time to read, because they are already targets for innumerable committees, associations, pressure groups and public bodies. If they have some special interest in a particular part of the Third World, their requirements usually are satisfied by material predigested for them by their assistants, which consists of stuff far more solid than the newsletters of missions.

There are already so many missions in any capital of the developed world that these people tend to feel suffocated by publications and regard their coming more as a nuisance than as a convenience. Furthermore, the higher bureaucrats and parliamentarians prefer to read the reports of their own diplomats in Third-World countries. They consider these surer guides than the emanations of those countries' embassies in their capitals. To beam newsletters to them is preaching not to the converted, but to the conversant, who have already decided how they will interpret what has been reported to them. This therefore is much labour lost unless the presentation is especially adroit.

A mission that decides instead to aim at the intelligentsia will usually have made the wise choice. Not only is it a broader group, spread through many professions and advocations, it is also the group that organizes the pressures on the political system, local, regional and national, that is professionally in close touch with large numbers of people, and that constitutes the membership of clubs, lodges, associations and unions across the land. These are people who avidly follow the national and international news to see how the current of events affects them. These are people who read more than just their newspapers. They will generally study an article with care if it arouses their interest or provokes their sensibilities.

The *cognoscente* are always hoping to win over large sections of the intelligentsia to their particular causes, because the latter are crucial in the strategy of permeation. By permeation I mean the filtering through a society of ideals on which the governing group wants to act but for which it first wants to be certain of broad support. Not all the intelligentsia are opinion formers and not all opinion formers are members of the intelligentsia. But this group forms a sort of bridge between the governors and their strategies, and the governed and their susceptibilities. The concerns of the intelligentsia are usually both narrower and wider than those of their leaders. Narrower because they often look at politics from the angle of particular avocations; broader because they often have a more exacting concept of political behaviour than their representatives find comfortable.

Third-World missions pondering readership for their publications could hardly do better than aim at the intelligentsia. If those publications are well written and laid out, they are likely to be read by at least some of the intelligentsia. Those who have an interest in a particular Third-World country will be readers. So will those who, seeing the fragility of the international environment, are concerned about the shape of things to come and feel compelled to look beyond the confines of their own country for continuing security. Insecurity often has two distinctly opposite effects. The first is that people form smaller and more tightly knit circles for protection; the second is that they enlarge their perceptions and their ambit to control the factors that make them insecure. It is to the latter of these types that intelligently written productions from the Third-World missions will appeal.

When a mission decides to publish a newsletter, having picked upon its potential readership, it must decide editorial style. The newsletter, to be persuasive rather than polemical, must follow certain lines. To begin, the publishers might consider four functions.

First, the newsletter exists to change an outlook. Its tone must therefore be cool and reasonable and it must link the wellbeing of the reader with that of those on whose behalf it is being written. For instance, commentary on the sore points of the present world order should be in compelling detail, without accusatory bursts of rage, sarcasm or epithets. Details should enable readers to identify with the problem: say the cost of a tin of sardines in relation to the selling price of a kilo of rice, or the strong rise in the price of tractors compared with the modest rise or even decline in that of sisal. When it points out that those who are forced to sell their products low cannot buy tractors and sardines, the reader can identify through these examples with the condition. He can see the problem it raises for his own economic future as well as the injustices, written into the system, that it inflicts on others.

The newsletter should challenge the myth of the international free market. For many in the developed societies the free market is an article of faith, seen as necessary not only for the economic salvation of their own societies, but for that of the globe as a whole. Taking the trade patterns of its own society, the embassy publication should demonstrate how unfree the system really is. The great transnational corporations can block the play of market forces. The price of primary products is kept so low that they cannot contribute to the development thrust of the country, while the price of needed imports from the developed world is kept so high as to drain away foreign reserves. The publication should subtly demonstrate this by letting the evidence speak for itself.

Labour in developed societies is often frustrated in its organized pressure on the transnationals by the use of sweated labour in developing societies. This calls for an explanation to trade-union leaders of the way a common damage is done to labour in the Third and First Worlds. This appeal to their self-interest is sure to have a telling impact on them.

The second function of such a publication is to correct false impressions. The most important of these is that poor countries do little by themselves to allay their condition, spending their own scarce resources or those allotted to them by donor countries on prestige projects that do more to glorify nationalism than to transcend poverty. Here the publication will be an educator of its audience, telling of the immense effort the Third World has made, albeit with puny results. The publication will contrast government with non-government efforts, highlighting instances where communities of people rise up to help themselves without the vast machinery of government and showing where government has been the catalyst, but not the operator, of projects involving large numbers of people.

There is a special reason for presenting this balance. Throughout the Western world one finds a paradox: people make tremendous demands on government while solemnly disliking government interference. The fear of an all-powerful state is matched by the demands for an all-providing state; the more the state mounts the machinery of social security, the greater the cry is of too much government. This psychological ambivalence must be recognized by the editors and writers of newsletters. Too much attention to government activity and they will lose the interest (or even stir up the hostility) of those who fear the encroaching power of the state. But if they balance the news of self-help among ordinary people with news of government activities to assist those people, they will find a sympathetic response within the Western breast. Besides, as any good journalist will confirm, stories of self-help, of poor people making a breakthrough without large handouts, make good copy. Such items are human; as challenge and response they satisfy the Western devotion to initiative, and they show how much the poor do to break the stranglehold of deprivation.

It is also crucial for the newsletter to demonstrate the thought, creativity, energy and skill that many Third-World governments apply to the problems of underdevelopment. These qualities, vigorously alive in the developing world, must be shown as vital preconditions for most of the small, incremental gains made in development. It demands careful writing, for it is easy to fall into the trap of rhapsodizing a government merely because it exists – and of overstating what it actually does and understanding what small people do under its umbrella. But the care taken will be rewarded in the message of intelligent use of scarce resources and the fostering of self-reliance at individual and national levels.

The third function of an embassy publication should be to clear up misunderstandings that might otherwise increase hostility toward Third-World countries. For instance, the policy of import substitution widely practised by Third-World countries is much misunderstood. Many Western societies see this as deliberate interference with the free market, or at the very least as aimed at destroying 'sensible' commercial relations with Western countries. Here, a newsletter can dispel a number of myths conveniently assembled under one roof: the myth of the incapacity of the Third World to produce food and the myth that the import of 'cheap' food frees local energies for more important tasks of development.

A newsletter must establish first that the production of food for local consumption is a prime duty of poor countries if general starvation is to be avoided; dependence on the granaries of the developed world is no solution to this problem. Second, it must establish that the potential for food production in the Third World is far greater than normally assumed by those in the rich countries, who are accustomed to being told that developing nations can either export raw materials or feed themselves but not both at the same time. Third, the newsletter will show that when countries of the Third World grow their own food to feed their own people (as well as attempting to export some of it) they promote the stabilization of their societies. They create within themselves a model of the economic order they are demanding outside.

To communicate such information takes imagination and expertise. This may be a description of an economic development, but it should be told as a human story. The reader must feel what it means to the local small farmer to have his produce needed and bought and what it means to low-income people, particularly the children, to have nutritious food available. Finally, the newsletter will show what it means to have formerly untilled land brought into the service of the nation, thereby obviating the need to find foreign exchange for imports of food that, being insufficient or expensive, left the mass of people underfed.

There is the story of cassava and the experiments (under the auspices of international bodies such as, for instance, the International Development Research Centre) that reduced its poison content and introduced protein content. It makes good reading, and not only to those interested in the human aspects of it. Increased fish culture in some developing countries – for example, Guyana – combined with a revolution in local tastes, leading to a greater consumption of fish, is another story for a newsletter. For fish is an excellent source of protein; most developed nations are great consumers of it. The news that some developing societies are turning to this most natural resource will strike a sympathetic chord in the minds of readers.

The fourth function for a publication of this sort is to spotlight areas of co-operation between the country in which it is issued and the country about which it is written. The agencies concerned with helping developing societies in one way or another often need an understanding public to back their efforts. Such bodies have their critics. These either affect not to understand what they are doing or take the view that development aid amounts to ploughing the sand at the expense of the donor country's taxpayers, who should either be relieved of such burdens or see the resources more fruitfully deployed at home. A newsletter that explains the contributions to development of these agencies in conjunction with bodies in its own country is not expressing pious gratitude but conducting an exercise in intelligent self-interest.

But as in so many other things journalistic, the manner of doing is as important as the fact that it is done. A headline, 'Canada allocates $25 million for forestry development', followed by a description of negotiations for the grant and the way it would be spent, with a picture of the signing ceremony, will produce more critics than supporters.

What's needed is an article depicting the likely results of this grant on the internal economic life of the country or on its external trade; one that shows how the people involved and the land they live in will be affected. This, with sensitively selected illustrations, is more likely to catch the eye, arouse the interest and evoke the support of internationally minded readers. Announcements by development agencies in Western countries about their own successes are frequently received by the media with scepticism or silence. When developing countries indicate what growth the contributions of those agencies have stimulated and what legitimate spinoffs have accrued, the media are more likely to believe. This helps to create a climate of mutuality, which will render more acceptable the often necessary criticisms of the trade policies of developed countries. Thus the newsletter strikes a balance between highlighting what is unjust and focusing on what is intelligent, and it keeps the door open for continued dialogue on the world economic order.

A further guideline for a newsletter is variety. It should be given sparkle by touches of humour that illustrate the moods and mores of the people. Almost everyone is turned on by humour. It should indicate the continuing vibrancy of the society even in the face of its gigantic problems. It should also illustrate the continuing vitality and resourcefulness within the society despite the economic conditions. Items on the culture of the country, especially the culture people create to deal with their own limitations, will attract readers – there are a lot of people not interested in the complexities of development who are interested in culture. They may begin by looking only at those items and end by reading the rest.

These inclusions will add colour and tone to the newsletter without making it an advertisement whose plushness contradicts its message.

Finally it is important to invoke the historical experience of the society to which the publication is addressed. With the aid of historians and social scientists it can establish a kinship between the readers and Third-World peoples. A reference, for example, to the depression of the 1930s in Europe and North America can still stir memories.

The newsletter can draw a parallel between the case for developing societies and the case for regional development policies within developed nations. Emphasizing the principle of equal opportunity (which, to the peoples of the rich countries, is so fundamental an article of faith that it has become an emotion more than a belief) is a useful strategy; that, it may be pointed out, is all the Third World is asking for – an unrevolutionary demand taken straight out of First-World experience. The newsletter that demonstrates this will exorcise what many people see to be the demon in Third-World proposals. Indeed, if there is one thread that could run through all the issues of the newsletter, as it deals with different facets of the home society, it is the fundamentally conservative nature of the demands of the Third World for a new international economic order.

A publication based on these guidelines will have one further great advantage. It will greatly assist development education groups within developed societies to persuade their own countrymen of the wisdom, if not necessarily the morality, of a move toward international reconstruction.

Finally, there should be occasions when the newsletter demonstrates what the Third World is doing to help itself. A regional association of developing states can make a powerful impact on the intelligentsia by issuing, for some special occasion, a joint publication. This would concentrate on what the regional institutions are doing within each territory to exploit resources, train manpower, integrate economies and raise the level of development thinking. Such a collective effort must be carefully co-ordinated and well written. It will then counter the widespread impression in developed countries that even neighbouring Third-World countries have at best a collective devotion to their own disunity. Such occasional issues make a telling case for more amenable approaches to global rethinking. They point out what results flow from regional efforts and how much more would be jointly achieved under a better-structured international order.

A collective publication is likely to have the greatest impact in the European Economic Community. It is here, where regionalism has scored some of its most material successes, that recommendations to Third-World nations for collective behaviour come trippingly off the tongue.

Before we conclude this exposition of guidelines, however, a note of caution: the issues should certainly be published regularly (some major event, no doubt, is worth a special edition) but not with encumbering frequency. Creative and skilful productions need time and talent. Weak inputs will mean only weak outputs, which can have only two effects: bored readers and then no readers.

Many developing countries are not short of first-rate journalists. What those journalists are short of is the opportunity to be read by thinking people in the developed countries. Quality, and sometimes its reverse, in First-World journalism gets every opportunity to extend itself to the Third World. There are fellowships for those who wish to spend up to a year in developing societies, observing their policies, their patterns of production and consumption and their political behaviour. In addition, not surprisingly, the great news corporations sell their stories and reports throughout the developing world on the basis of the coverage that their money and manpower can ensure. As a result the Third World still reads far more of the First World than the First World even reads of the Third. In fact it would be nearer to the point to say that while the Third World is often impressively knowledgeable about the First, the First World is too often depressingly ignorant about the Third.

It is not only about events – cataclysmic, climacteric and

constructive – that the First World needs to know from the Third. Far more than that, it needs to learn about the sheer human ingenuity characteristic of the efforts of developing countries. It needs to know a lot more about the heroic men and women who spend long, weary hours trying to work out answers to problems that bedevil them. These are people who patiently teach villagers defeated by circumstance how to try less back-breaking methods of production, people who resourcefully adapt technology to the needs of rural areas or give to old, simple technology new and more fertile uses. Most of all, the First World needs to know about the implications, for itself and its much smaller sector of mankind, of escalating misery. In a word, those of the First World need to come to terms with a future that promises them less security than that to which they feel entitled.

One way to disturb the complacency that insulates many inhabitants of the rich countries is the presence of distinguished Third-World journalists among them. Such people are usually clear and realistic about their own environment and can express their knowledge cogently but not abrasively. They can thus implant in the minds of their readers a receptivity to the alternative lexicon and the vision that it implies.

Ambassadors must play a central role in organizing this kind of exchange. If their relations with leading journalists or media institutions in the host country are close, they can arrange to have one of their country's leading writers or broadcasters appointed for a time to the staff of one of the more enlightened newspapers or broadcasting stations. The duty of the visiting practitioner would be to prepare special features on aspects of the Third World underreported by the media of the developed societies. It is an axiom of the media that almost any subject can be made compelling if skilfully presented. To Western people, of course, the rhythms and lifestyles of the Third World are not in themselves eye-catching. Also, accustomed to hearing about their coups and counter-coups, Westerners often unreflectingly adopt Trevor-Roper's attitude toward the affairs of Third-World peoples, that they are the unrewarding gyrations of barbarous peoples in picturesque but irrelevant corners of the globe.[11]

Poverty, to those accustomed to excitement, seems a depressing subject. It is therefore the difficult task of a visiting media person to turn these attitudes round. He or she must encourage interest and receptivity, and then link the receptivity to an understanding of the need for change. What the media visitor has to his advantage is a deep, personal knowledge of one or more developing societies, and the nature of human experience in those places. That, if adroitly presented, can intrigue almost any audience, which is the first stage of becoming involved.

If the established media are not interested in hosting Third-World writers (and this has to be expected in some countries), the possibilities are not exhausted. There are departments of journalism in most major Western universities. An ambassador with an entrée to university circles can negotiate the appointment of a quality journalist from his country as a visiting professor of journalism. The function of the visitor will be, of course, to teach, to hold seminars with students and members of faculty. But in so doing he will, if sufficiently skilled, be dwelling not only on method but on content or, to use a more professional word, on meaning. For instance, he will point to the different criteria used by writers of the First World, when reporting events in their own regions, from those they use when reporting events in his. He will highlight the dichotomy by which a writer seeks to understand poverty within his own society but dismisses it as the result of fecklessness or corruption in developing ones. He will also point out the contradiction by which a liberal journalist welcomes organizations by ordinary people to promote their interests in developed societies, while condemning such national organizations in the developing world. In fact his major job will be to clarify the hidden assumptions of much First-World journalism in relation to the Third.

I said that his primary duty would be with his university appointment. That does not mean that he will be exclusively preoccupied by it. There are also opportunities for beaming his message to a larger constituency through daily newspapers, weekly journals, radio and television. As a professional journalist – and not merely an academic teacher of journalism – his network of contacts will extend beyond the university campus. These contacts will bring him openings to put the Third-World case in a way that is sophisticated and still palatable.

Provided, that is, he understands the preferred vocabulary of the society and uses it skilfully in introducing the alternative lexicon. If he understands the audience for which he is writing, he can invoke their standards of justice and enlightened self-interest and relate them to the world at large. If he knows their apprehensions he can tot up for his readers' benefit his balance sheet, showing how much they have to gain by understanding the world's needs. It is, of course, probable that he will be asked to write only for dailies and journals that are politically middle-of-the-road or left-of-centre. But he may also be asked to write for religious publications with concerns for greater international equality. Even if he is not a religious person, such an opportunity should not be foregone. At the very least, his approach will help the journal in its strategies of persuasion.

The increasing activities of journalists from the Third World in developed societies is bound to have a kindling effect. At the very minimum, some people from those societies will be exposed to a new interpretation of the news they see and hear. That could begin a shift of perspective as great as that now occurring in the developing countries. This two-way stream will not only make Third-World countries more receptive to journalists from the First, it will establish a fundamental mutuality.

When the Third World becomes accustomed to hearing about itself from itself, it will be more inclined to listen to what the First World says about it. And when the two worlds journal-istically begin to exchange their perceptions, you have the basis for a dialogue that can take both sides further than the North–South débâcle has been able to do. India has been an exemplary, keeping in London a number of distinguished Indian journalists who understand enough of British psychology to talk meaningfully to their British readership. As this chapter suggests, other countries could be doing the same, even if by different arrangements.

5 Pedagogues and Practitioners: Diplomats and the Universities

There is a widespread conviction that ambassadors and universities are mutually exclusive. The milieu of the former is thought to be secrecy, equivocation, tentativeness, evasion and a devotion to absolutes masked by a vocabulary of relatives, whereas the milieu of the latter is clarity, integrity, audacity, pugnacity and liberty of thought and expression.

There are those who say that the two trades have nothing in common, and that friction can be the only result of their encounter. Ambassadors are believed to dislike universities because their indigenes ask them to explain too much, and universities are believed to distrust ambassadors because the latter give away too little. Long experience has taught those in public life that the servants of an inflexible position are never its best exponents. This defect is frequently ascribed to diplomats, and diplomats who do not enjoy the university atmosphere assert that those who live in a world of theory do not understand a world of reality.

And so the myths on either side proliferate.

They proliferate to the point that many diplomats and academics will not deal with each other except in very formal ways that allow almost no personal interchange. Between them there is rarely any dialogue – not even the type described as the dialogue of the deaf. True, ambassadors frequently invite academics to their cocktail parties and academics reciprocate by inviting ambassadors to their functions. But reciprocity of alcohol does not necessarily mean a reciprocity of communication.

Those ambassadors who believe in bolstering their mystique will obviously enter universities only for those formal occasions where a speech has to be made with no questions asked. It would not do to have His Excellency questioned and found wanting, which would only tarnish the considerable prestige of the corps as a whole and the ambassador's country in particular. Better to retain one's reputation by keeping the cordon sanitaire around oneself than to transgress the safety line and confirm the scepticism that many academics harbour about diplomats.

These attitudes are real and in some countries widespread. But they can be and often are overplayed and are really irrelevant to the world as it is likely to be in the last two decades of the twentieth century. For the Third-World ambassador in particular, universities are of seminal significance. Ambassadors from developing countries cannot afford any longer to sustain the myths and the mystique that in former times and in older societies surrounded their counterparts.

The ritual of sovereignty – asserting and demonstrating it – has now its full play. Its value lay in underscoring the legal equality of all nations. When it was new, the time and energy spent on declaring it was legitimate. But it is now a fact of international life, and the world has become accustomed to seeing the former subjects of empire as their own masters. They need no longer flourish the trumpets to prove that they are there.

But they do have a long, painful, patient campaign before them – the campaign to alter the structured inequality of the present global system. With the degenerating conditions of the developing world, assertions of sovereignty are less important than the attempt to alter people's thinking and stimulate new lines of action.

In this struggle for survival with dignity, perception is as important as economics. For the bottom of the problem is not merely a calculation of dollars, but a clash of ways of looking at the world. In short, those who want things to remain as they are have a perception of the globe's future that cannot be shared by those who are urgent for change. For instance one side says: 'If the poor *will* themselves to limit their numbers, they can palpably diminish their poverty.' The other side says: 'If the rich *will* themselves to alter the structures that make millions poor, the latter will have no problem in limiting their numbers.'

The battle over the equitable distribution of the earth's resources is fundamentally a battle of visions. It follows, therefore, that universities, those quickeners of perception, are crucial to the outcome. Universities do not ignore the problem of structural change. They may decide against it or for it, but they are always looking at it. To be more precise, certain departments are always looking at it and inviting their students to do so.

But before we explore the relationship between Third-World ambassadors and universities in the countries of their posting, let us pause and look at universities as a whole. There are three aspects of any university that are important to the Third-World ambassador: its relationship to the whole world, its relationship to the local political structure and its relationship to the future.

The first characteristic, then, that concerns us is the idea that a community of academics is an international reality going beyond ideological divisions, national myopias and provincial prejudices. The university transcends – at least in theory – both the nation-state and confessional collectivities. It is the local and visible sign of an international, intellectual entity. It is nothing if it is not more than local, and everything if it is both local and international.

This is historical. European universities, which in one way or another have been the model for all others, were founded before the nation-state was born. They were conceived in theology and dedicated to the proposition that all truth was created universal. They were concerned with an ordering of the world that corresponded with the ordering of truth. It was necessary to be universal to be intelligently particular.

Modern universities in their stated ideals (if not always in their practice) preserve this original concept. Truth is indivisible, they proclaim, even when they add *sotto voce* that it is essentially American or French or Russian or Chinese. This old ideal, this concept of essence, has nowadays a new validity or indeed a new urgency.

For it means that by a peculiar paradox universities have been both behind the times and ahead of them. Behind, because in a fragmented world of nation-states and ideological cleavages, they have seemed intractably old-fashioned in their continuing devotion to the international community of scholars. Ahead because, though some have stubbornly refused to recognize the intimate interdependence of the world of the twentieth century, others have been grasping at it – sometimes faintly and sometimes very clearly – ahead of their political community. Indeed in a number of them there have continuously been the glimmerings of

the global vision behind the provincial cloudbanks. Some of the
most distinguished academics in East and West have been brave
enough to assert the oneness of the world at the expense of their
promotion or their freedom of movement.

The second characteristic is the relationship between
universities in the developed world and their local political
structures. Basically it is one of ambiguity, of distance carefully
maintained and of utility carefully cultivated. Academics insist
on preserving their freedom to think, speculate, research and
criticize. They also expect to be called on to assist governments
with their planning, their programming and even their attempts
at persuasion. Some, notably Henry Kissinger, go from the groves
of academe, where they gave advice to political figures, straight
to the centres of power, where they execute policies. Others go
from politics, where they made decisions, to academia, where
they teach how decisions are made. Universities are frequently
the mistresses of governments, but governments are not always
their masters. There is a reserve about universities even when they
are giving service – a peculiar combination of attachment and
detachment. The numerous apologists for this situation describe
it as creative tension; they say it springs from the knowledge that
the political and academic orders have a great need of each other,
but that need should not blur the distinction between their
spheres.

The difference in situation between an academic and a politician contributes to considerable misunderstanding. For one
thing, the academic has time on his side and the politician has
time as his enemy. It is easier for the academic to distinguish the
wood from the trees, because the pressures to decide are not
eternally upon him. It is easier for the politician to understand
the decision-making process, because he feels the pressures from
all sides, which the academic does not. Politicians are therefore
frequently irritated with the academics' distaste for their
adhocracies. Academics are as frequently irritated with the
politicians' insistence on the virtues of sheer survival. But their
mutual irritation is just another facet of their mutual fascination.
The one lives in a state of urgency but needs a sense of depth. The
other lives by probing the depths but lacks a sense of urgency. It is
vital for diplomats from the Third World to appreciate this
dialectical relationship between academics and politicians in
Western societies.

In the ambiguous relationships between the universities and the political order in developed societies, there is a valid lesson for developing countries. The course of campus–government relationships, like that of true love, never does run smooth, and so many Third-World governments have decided that the only good university is an 'obedient' one. They hold that scholarship is more confirmatory than explorative, that government is there to supply the thesis and the university to supply the proof, that distance between the two entities amounts to the disloyalty of one of them, and that when resources are scarce independent judgement buttressed by patient research is not an affordable luxury.

Ambassadors who have observed the ambiguity and ambivalence between universities and the authorities in rich societies can, with tact and penetration, bring their own governments to a less spartan view of university usefulness. They can help their political directorates to appreciate the ground-breaking work of academics. When not obligated to sign declarations of fashionable piety, scholars of commitment and integrity can play sometimes anticipatory, sometimes admonitory, often advisory roles.

Ambassadors can also remind governments that they cannot afford universities that merely footnote policies subsequently found at great expense to be inadequate. For the politicians will quickly turn for advice to more independent sources – which of course will be outside the country. This, then, will be the net result (and probably an expensive and embarrassing one) of denying the Third-World university its true potential in the interests of short-term convenience.

But the value of observing the dialectic between universities and politicians in Western countries lies not only in the lessons to be learned for home consumption, but in what it can contribute to the day-to-day practice of diplomacy. Academics can be a channel through which politicians and diplomats send messages to one another outside the normal courses of bureaucracy.

This is particularly useful when both sides are looking for a fuller picture on which to base a decision or a recommendation. The politician, while not undervaluing his bureaucracy, may want to supplement its analysis with that of others; the diplomat may want some idea of how discussion on alternatives is going so that he can make discreet inputs without face-to-face communication.

Ambassadors who have the respect and intimacy of those

academics who advise political figures will (the politicians being agreeable) exchange helpful insights with them. This method has distinct advantages for both sides: the politician can absorb from the diplomat, via the academic, information sharpened by an insider's knowledge; the ambassador on his side can receive soundings over possible policies to test his government's feelings. No commitment is implied either way, because the tentative and oblique approach implies no official recognition. The academic can thus be helpful in preserving the propriety of relationships while helping the exploration of possibilities.

The third characteristic of universities of importance to Third-World ambassadors is their concern with the future. They have an interest in technology – the application of mechanical power to human needs. But increasingly, as the results of the unchecked use of technology become clear, universities are looking at the ecological balance, of the threat to his own survival that man poses to himself by the pillage of the earth's resources. This is an area of concern in universities in which the Third-World representative has an understandably great interest. To dominate the earth is, in many university circles, less prudent, even less sane, than to use its energies in a harmonious way. The search for a technology that does not deplete the earth but completes its rhythms is rapidly becoming legitimate as pure self-interest. To use less fossil fuel and more solar or wind energy is now no longer an idea of the lunatic fringe, as it appeared to be just over a decade ago. Of course those who espouse these alternatives still are fewer than those who lust for earth mastery. But in general, their numbers in universities are growing, and the Third-World ambassador must take note of their existence and make their acquaintance.

The universities show concern for the future also in their analysis of world economic trends. The worry over a possible shift in affluence is at the bottom of this rigorous activity, and one can see the possibility of two results of this worry: negative-minded defence of the wealth of the West or a positive realization that the wealth of the West cannot be maintained at the expense of the poverty of others.

One effect that the concern for the future has on the universities of the rich countries is to lift them out of a cuddling parochialism. For the pressure to serve only a local constituency, especially if that is where most of the funding comes from, is very strong on universities. So is the pressure to reserve university places only for the sons and daughters of the area, thereby excluding students from the developing world, a problem that is becoming more widespread and one that Third-World ambassadors will have to face.

Universities everywhere create climates of opinion. They are not the only creators, nor at any prevailing point in time the most potent influence. But where the impact of the media is ephemeral, that of universities is more enduring. They produce generations of opinion as opposed to stampedes of reaction. Each university forms an intellectual environment in which there are prevailing winds and minor currents, fashionable orthodoxies and equally fashionable heterodoxies; from all this their graduates form the concepts from which they draw as they exercise power or influence.

But most important of all, universities are places where intellectual minorities can flourish without the heavy social penalties that the larger society tends to impose on them. Part of the reason for this is the sacred notion of the value of dissent common to all liberal societies of the West. Part of it is the conviction that maturity makes conservatives of us all – that yesterday's campus radicals are today's corporate managers. Better, say the apologists for the universities, that the passions of apocalypse be spent in student politics than explode into national ones.

The universities of the rich societies will therefore give a hearing to the diplomats from the Third World if they are global in their exposition, non-sulphurous in their presentation and penetrating in their message. In short, the diplomat's case must appeal both to the self-interest as well as the sense of scholarship of those whom they address. In this theatre, size and clout count for less than in most other areas of national life. Faculty and students generally prefer listening to a lucid ambassador from a small developing country than to one from a weighty developed country who merely reiterates the already known pronouncements of his principals at home. In that valuable sense, universities are a truly democratic forum where the small and less-known are equal with the large and the better-known; the frequency of their invitations will depend on the quality of their presentations. So an ambassador has to earn any respect he gets in a university; it comes neither with the country he represents nor with the status he holds.

It is imperative that Third-World ambassadors and their senior staff grasp this opportunity. First, it underscores the seriousness of their commitment to structural change if they advocate it in person before critical audiences. Sending their underlings (say a lower-echelon information officer) to perform the task for them is seen by students and faculty as denigrating the importance of the university; the reaction is predictably dismissive. Or worse, they assume that the ambassador or his minister-counsellor is not up to the task of serious discussion with trained minds on global problems. Even a skilful information officer is no substitute for the ambassador or one of his senior colleagues – not where it is a matter of talking to faculty or students at a higher level. Also the general assumption (not far wrong) is that the information officer is the embassy propaganda machine, programmed to paint the picture from only one perspective and not equipped to discuss the issues in a discursive and argumentative forum.

Much of the really crucial background work on the North–South dialogue (crucial in the sense that the South's case is carefully and trenchantly documented) has been done by universities in the developed world. S. S. Ramphal has clearly, if to the surprise of many, pointed this out.[12] As he puts it, the work that has been done has been to establish the intellectual premises of North–South co-operation, which is after all the start for any meaningful dialogue. Those engaged in this task naturally look for active, personal support from the ambassadors of developing countries, who flesh out the case they make and add not only supportive information but personal insight.

The ambassador and his senior staff may, of course, bring emphases to the corpus of thought that differ somewhat from those of the academic researchers. But their frequent visits and continuing consultation with the researchers are valuable for both sides, especially as ambassadors and their staff can often go where academics cannot and academics can often go where ambassadors and their staffs do not.

In their dealings with academics, representatives from developing countries will be able to distinguish three broad categories with interests in development.

The first consists of those whose only concern is their professional survival or promotion. They must publish or perish, and the Third World offers eminently publishable opportunities, especially for economists, political scientists, anthropologists, sociologists, historians or literary critics. They will indeed publish. Others meantime will perish.

Second are those whose concern is both academic and personal. They are appalled by the plight of the poor. They oppose continuing structural imbalance in the global order and look for ways to change it. Publication is not professionally less important for them, but its function is subsumed in a larger purpose: to contribute to the discussion on poverty and instability and offer thoughtful advice to those working for change. Their publications tend to be scholarly but committed, rigorous but practical. They publish that others may not perish.

The third group comprises those academics actually involved with the Third World. Some are advisers to universities in the developing world; some have been members of Third-World faculty; others are consultants to governments or advisers on non-government projects. Because most of these academics have actually lived and worked in Third-World countries, they maintain an interest not only in the areas where they lived, but in development issues as a whole. They often join those from the second category to form pressure groups for Third-World interests within their campuses and also in larger political circles. Frequently they are called on by the media for background to events in the countries where they lived. Their publications show a wealth of inside knowledge and a sense of the local culture that short visits, however well intentioned, cannot yield.

An ambassador and his staff, if they are astute, will see through the protestations and discover who are the group one types and will not spend more time with them than is socially necessary – especially as their publications are often unsympathetic to changes of the sort proposed by the developing world. With groups two and three they will, of course, have close contact. The ambassador can reasonably expect help in the form of the results of their latest research. Often they will defend his country from the misinformation of intransit 'experts'. This could, for instance, mean replying to an article in one of the local or national newspapers or magazines. The accuracy and intimacy of their knowledge is far more credible in refuting misrepresentations than the routine reply of an embassy official, which generally cannot be expected to carry much conviction.

There is yet another university group, which for obvious reasons is not classed with the others, that in the last twenty-five years has grown considerably: Third-World academics who have migrated to Western countries. Of these, some have burned their metaphorical boats behind them and take no further interest in their birthplaces; others continue to be concerned personally and academically with developments at home and are willing to make contributions with the skills at their disposal. Not only do they write sympathetically and sensitively about the country, but they can sometimes be persuaded to lend their services as consultants. In a number of instances, they have devoted whole sabbaticals to this kind of service, an extremely valuable form of technical co-operation, particularly if their skills are much in demand in the home country and if the government is relieved of the burden of a full salary.

In fact this is one of the most productive aspects of the relationship between universities of the West and those of the South, and there is much room for expansion. And a Third-World academic, returning home under this kind of agreement, is immediately effective, which saves a lot of time, discomfort and even embarrassment.

But it is not only with highly technical and experienced researchers that ambassadors should communicate. Every university in the developed world has a corps, sometimes large, sometimes tiny, of students devoted to an internationalism that is consonant with Third-World perspectives. These students may not always be fully informed; none the less they are frequently opinion-formers on campus, having a voice, a vogue and a political vocation. Some of them quietly influence others; they meet in small groups to consider the plight of the wretched and look not so much for palliatives as for avenues to change. Others are more zealous than well-briefed, spoiling their case by overkill when they could promote it by sober understatement.

But whatever their techniques they deserve a diplomat's notice. And not only notice but actually encouragement and advice on how to present their case. The visit of an ambassador, a counsellor or even a press secretary to one of these groups boosts their influence. The diplomat's advice on presentations will not only serve an immediate purpose but also give them an education in political persuasion. Once the contact with the officer from the embassy is made, the mission can then send these groups material for their needs. Again, this is for both their own education and that of their fellow-students. Thus the embassy casts its bread upon the waters. For though campus fashions change and vogues go out of style, those who as students clearly understand the South's case and the value to the North of the viability of the South will take that with them into their professions and avocations.

Some will take the moral issue and remain advocates for global reconstruction on that level. Others will take with them the economic considerations and the hard-headed calculations they involve. A few will follow the political approach. What is important is that they work as part of their nation's life rather than from the outside. As they learn the language of their chosen professions the will also learn how to use that language to raise the global consciousness of their colleagues. But this brings us back to what we said earlier: with students two things are required to kindle attraction. The first is to engage their minds, which is the first purpose of their being at university. The second is to engage their desire to be on the side of the future. For with students more than with most others, vindication by the future is the *raison d'être* of the present.

Universities almost uniquely mingle the intransigently parochial and the liberally international. There are those for whom the future is a matter of careers. These are inevitably the great majority. But there are others who for a variety of reasons (not the least of which is that their parents lived abroad or worked with global networks of one sort or another) cannot think in purely local terms. Such students are not necessarily radical or even left-of-centre. But their consciousness is larger than they would achieve purely by focusing on a career.

Some will become important in civic affairs, others in provincial life and a few will become significant as national personalities. But at every level it is crucial that what they take with them from university is a sense of viable alternatives to the present international order. That means a grasp of programmes that make alternatives available and a grasp of tactics to make the programmes workable.

This kind of student will know that the Third World has alternatives that are not violent, rabid or sectarian, that do not demand the impoverishment of the North for the survival of the South, and that assume the comfortable survival of the globe as a whole. From this point he will persuade his fellows to take a less provincial view of the world.

But the students just described are not all of those to whom the news of a new kind of global community will come as a gospel. In every university of the developed world are numbers who call themselves the alienated. They do not feel at one with the ethos or ethics of their society (whether on campus or in the whole of the Western culture) and seek another and better way of life. Some of these turn to meditation, nurturing the spirit to transcend the structures. They seek domains of reality beyond this; mental levitation is their release. Others grasp for an ideology of societal change, a blueprint for a new order in which there is neither class conflict nor competitiveness.

Both groups feel deep unease about the present local and international distribution of power and money. Both would like to live in a differently ordered world. One – the group of those who try to overcome alienation from within – does not believe that structural change is possible; the system is too malevolent, irreversible. The other believes that, as by man came the present structures, by man also can come the alteration of those structures. But there is a revealing link between the two groups. The spiritual exercises the first group practises come from those parts of the world that demand change; the profound structural changes the second group envisages are global rather than sectoral. For to them the South is the world's proletariat whose poverty makes possible the comfort of the North, the world's bourgeoisie. To the first group salvation comes from light rising up in the South. To the second group the restructuring comes from the imperatives the suffering of the South has created.

The link between the two is very important for a Third-World diplomat. For he, too, represents alienation – the alienation of millions from the international economic and political system, which rewards them only with deprivation. He can point out to both groups that two opposite causes produce the same condition. In the rich North, alienation comes from the competitive waste of scarce resources. In the South it comes from the unavailability of the resources that are pre-empted elsewhere. The abuse in the one case and the unavailability in the other are deeply related. Neither the glutted nor the gutted have time or capacity for genuine civilization, which after all is the release of man from the tyranny of appetite for more reflective and organized activity.

It is on campuses that people look for analysis of the *malaises* that afflict them. It is in universities that (academic overspecialization apart) thoughtful students look for universals of thought. The Third-World ambassador presents a universal: the idea of a globe equitably organized for survival by the intelligent use of its resources. He turns the old ethical ideals of the world's religious systems into survival kits. It is now prudent to be moral and moral to be prudent.

If Third-World ambassadors are going to involve at least some universities in diplomatic activity, there should be some organization. To have members of the corps visiting universities at all is good, and the impact of one articulate diplomat is often astonishing The impact of a team of Third-World diplomats would be dynamic. The arrangement can be worked out in a number of ways. For instance, one of the peculiar strengths of an association like the Commonwealth is the continuing close dialogue between the developed and the developing members. The Commonwealth relationship is loose enough to allow members to participate in other international structures, yet tenacious enough for members to work together with an intimacy that makes co-operation creative and divergence frank.

A seminar on global problems staged by senior Commonwealth diplomats for faculty and students will not only demonstrate the nature of the association, but also the perspectives from which they approach international restructuring and the ways in which they co-operate with and help each other.

For instance, a discussion of the Commonwealth Fund for Technical Co-operation (CFTC), conducted by senior diplomats, would reveal much about the multinational approach to development. It would underline the premise on which the fund is based: that moderate but well-used resources can be more effective in development than bounteous funds deployed by an army of bureaucrats. Such a seminar would constitute a watershed in the thinking of many who may later be active in international affairs or involved in the conceptual thinking behind them. Projects of bodies like the CFTC use expertise from developing and developed countries, and the flow of skill does not move in one direction only; this will demonstrate to students and staff the actual workings of multilateral co-operation as well as the feeling of togetherness that accompanies them. To have a Sri Lankan, a Nigerian and a Jamaican advise the government of New Zealand on an energy project while a New Zealander, an Indian and a Canadian are advising the government of Guyana on a dairy project is a demonstration of the best kind of co-operation.

Students are concerned with examples as well as concepts, if only because when they come to write their examinations they need practical underpinnings. They suspect that Third-World co-operation is more a matter of passing resolutions than of real performance, and they ask constantly to be shown what is actually being done and how effective it is. They will not usually go and research these things for themselves, unless their graduate work requires it; even then they will be influenced in where to look for things by what they have heard from a country's representative. This is another reason that Third-World diplomats should go to universities. Their presentations, if lively and lucid, will not only ignite interest but also lead to a demand for resource materials at the department or departments.

Talking to an ambassador or a minister-counsellor is an unusual experience for students. On the one hand they feel the confidence of being on their own academic ground, free to make critical judgements. On the other hand they are talking to a practitioner – someone who every day puts the theories to test, who deals at an immediate level with complexities of policy. The world of theory looks different in the flesh, and sensitive and intelligent students are usually keen to see the relationship between the two domains. A stimulating diplomat can, while maintaining his professional discretion, help them to understand how the process works, meantime kindling their interest in the developing world and its philosophy of change.

But this example does not exhaust the possibilities of co-operation among ambassadors. Significant in the struggle for greater equality between the developed and developing worlds is the movement of non-aligned nations. It gets at best a contemptuous press in most of the rich societies. Its deliberations are usually treated as comic posturings. The movement is pictured as too divided to do anything but make noises and too dependent, ideologically or economically, on the rich countries to do anything but pass resolutions. Many students, even those in political science, have never heard of it. Some have heard of it but do not think it worth their attention. As a student once said to me: 'Why study a movement like the Christian calendar – it celebrates birth, agony and resurrection, interspersed by long periods of inactivity?'

It takes an encounter with someone versed in non-alignment to alter these attitudes. It is even better for a group of senior diplomats from countries heavily committed to the movement to explain its nature, aims and functioning, as well as its solid contribution to peace and stability. And this is best done by seminar – say with four ambassadors from non-aligned countries in different stages of development or in widely different regions. They can demonstrate the meaning of the movement for their societies and how it has engendered in the Third-World countries a realization that the solution to some of their problems and the beginnings of global change depend on their creating powerful organizations. But what needs to be demonstrated most of all is not the number of significant achievements that the movement has chalked up but the miracle of its very existence. Third-World countries can point to the pressure exerted on member countries to kill it. They can reveal the hostility to its aims of the great press agencies and the discrepancies between what they report and what actually happens. And they can discuss the policy of the North, which was first to ignore it, then to doubt its utility, and finally to credit anything it achieved to the wisdom of developed societies.

In the North generally and in universities particularly, it is a frequent complaint that representatives of developing countries are addicted to rhetoric rather than realism. They must dispel this misconception – and they can do it by comparison. They can demonstrate that practically all the great movements in the experience of Euro-American peoples have been accompanied by rhetoric. The great catalysts were rhetoricians of the first order, whether they came from the top or bottom of the social order and whether the changes were evolutionary or revolutionary. At least three distinct kinds of rhetoric have a long and vigorous record in the history of Europe and North America, especially since the eighteenth century, when expectation of change became a virtue rather than a sin.

There is the rhetoric of romance, which seeks to tranquilize men so that by dreams they bear ignoble realities. This is the rhetoric of obscurantist inertia, used by populists, demagogues and authoritarians who would maintain inherited privilege. Then there is the rhetoric of anger, in which a higher morality is invoked to damn social injustices but no clear alternatives are offered, just misty utopias. This is the rhetoric of angry imprecision. Finally there is a category of rhetoric that highlights the deficienies of a system that not only stunts the capabilities of its victims but saps the vitality of those who are supposed to be its beneficiaries. This kind of rhetoric does not, however, stop there. It offers alternatives, if not with exhaustive thoroughness at least with the colouring of human concern. This is the rhetoric of constructive passion, and its practitioners include Burke, Tom Paine, Lincoln, Talleyrand, Lenin, Clemenceau, F. D. Roosevelt, de Gaulle, Churchill, Nehru, Nkrumah, Willy Brandt, Martin Luther King – the line is long and distinguished.

What the ambassadors have to prove is that there is no necessary antithesis between rhetoric and programme. Great changes require vision and emotion as well as statistical rigour, and what the Third World now demands is so fundamental to the human species that all its sensibilities have to be engaged.

Apart from their presence, there are other ways in which diplomats could relate to institutions of higher learning in the countries of their posting.

The most important concerns the relations between universities of the First World and those of the Third. The relationship between the two has to date been much to the advantage of the former. Since the end of empire a stream of academics from developed countries has poured into the developing ones to help start faculties, temporarily to take senior posts, to give advice and of course to collect material for publication. Much of this has been at the invitation of young universities in the Third World. Taking the universities of developed countries as their model both in organization and in approach to the issues of their own societies (nowhere more visible than in their approach to development), they have sought the help of exponents within the older models.

For nearly two decades, development was expected to follow the path the rich societies had earlier trodden. It therefore seemed logical that academics from the North would be welcomed to set the process in operation. When academics from universities of developing countries went North for sabbaticals or postdoctoral fellowships, they were making their pilgrimages to the intellectual Meccas of the world. There they would absorb, steep themselves in the ethos of university life and equip themselves to return home as intellectual missionaries of the North. For the North's universities, it was a case of creation in one's own image, the purpose being to preserve and disseminate their value systems. The universities thus were, among other things, potent instruments of the Cold War.

Arrangements like the Fulbright scholarships were intended to ground academics from the developing countries in ideologies acceptable to the United States. This is turn would create universities whose ethos was Western if not slavishly American. The war for men's and women's minds would be won in the libraries, lecture halls and seminars of new universities in which the fervour must be Western. It was conceded as healthy that there be a national flavour – the insights of history, religion and society would reduce areas of conflict or upheaval that modernization inevitably brought, thereby preventing the inroads of communism. As for any idea that the South had something to teach the North about development, or that the models spawned by the rich had no relevance for the poor, or that the answers to world poverty might lie more with changes among the rich than among the poor – twenty years ago these notions would have seemed at best heretical and at worst absurd in university circles in the developed and developing worlds.

To some they still do. But some academics at not a few Western universities have come to reconsider. Doubts lead to new analyses of the world economic crisis. There is now a noticeable willingness to hear the men from the South. Streams now flow from South to North as well as North to South, and in this reversal ambassadors have a crucial part to play.

In universities with either institutes devoted to development studies or congeries of academics with developmental interests, an ambassador should try to arrange that one of the more distinguished academics from his own country spend a semester, if not a full academic year. At the least he or she could be invited to give a course of lectures. The presence of such academics from the developing world is more important than the lectures they give, for they come not to be trained as missionaries or to absorb an ethos, but to discuss approaches to a global problem in which neither side has all answers. Certainly they must offer the students and faculty a distillation of their thinking and research. But equally important is their input to courses on development issues, which frequently suffer from one-sidedness.

After all they live and think and work in the Third World. They can therefore contribute conceptual structures that those who frame such courses cannot easily arrive at, because they are looking at the subject from the outside in. The visitor will cull from his day-do-day experience in dealing with the development process concrete examples. Perspective is what will ultimately rank as his most valuable contribution – getting his students to see the case of the Third World as a global imperative involving the whole future of mankind and demonstrating to them the discrepancies between the beliefs the developed world proclaims and its actual performance – a very important point with those who live in the system and cannot see the discrepancies until they are pointed out.

There is no need here to stress unduly the spinoff effects. Such academics from the Third World will, in the natural course of things, identify academics in the universities they visit whose interest in the developing world is based on genuine sympathy. This will lead to return visits by them to Third-World countries where, with the assistance of their local colleagues, they can watch the development scene from within. The linkage also leads to a greater flow of material on the Third World to the universities of the First – a valuable contribution to a more balanced view.

The ambassador can also promote links between universities (or departments of universities) of the developed world and those of the developing world. These arrangements can be valuable to both sides. Highly specialized skills become available to the poor universities from the rich ones, and special insights become available to the rich universities from the poor ones. The universities of developed countries have much to offer, especially in areas like agriculture, food technology, fisheries, forestry, engineering and management. So too in the training of paramedics, nutritionists and media professionals. These are only some examples, possibly the most urgent, where co-operation between the two sets of universities can be beneficial to the developing worlds. And, through these special relationships, that co-operation is procured without the cumbersome apparatus of government-to-government relationships, which resemble the love-life of the elephant in that there is 'a great deal of trumpeting, everything done at the highest level and nothing to show for it for two years'. The mating of universities is not at all like that. As the budgets involved are restricted, there is little scope for waste, and personnel are employed in developing countries with care. Whereas their expertise is vital, they also learn to operate without the sophisticated technology to which they are accustomed.

The coupling of universities offers special opportunities for technological assistance, particularly to the universities of very small developing countries. Advanced universities in the rich world are the leading edge in technology. Therefore they often have a bank of less-than-current equipment, the disposal of which in their own society raises a few problems. On the other side of the great divide this equipment represents riches indeed. There, universities are operating with quite outdated equipment that may stretch the ingenuity of researchers but also slows them down. The transfer of equipment that in the First World is only slightly out-of-date to universities in small developing societies enables the recipients to do more in national development programmes. It also relieves a poor university of the need to spend its small budget on this equipment. This transfer, then, has the merit of answering two needs: on the one side disposal, on the other economy.

But of course the coupling of universities must offer mutual satisfaction. As academics from the universities of the North spend time in those of the South, so their counterparts from the South must spend time in the universities of the North. Not just for research, adding to the volume of written words more words of Southern wisdom to be stacked away in libraries, to be consulted by others doing the same thing. No, they must teach courses and conduct seminars, and if the university has what the British call an extramural department or what the North Americans call community outreach, they should be involved in that too, to reach a larger public.

In particular, academics from developing countries should concentrate their energies on schools of journalism (where they exist). This can have far-reaching consequences. First, their very presence makes them resource persons. Students looking for material for their projects or papers can ask for advice and thus have opened to them a new world with a perspective either unknown to them or known only by caricature. Second, the visitor will be able to help the students to look again at the assumptions about objectivity that govern so much developed-world reporting. Third, students will be led by the visitor to strip themselves of those attitudes, often implicit, that see the Third World as preachers not doers – that is, calling for changes in the international order while doing nothing about changes in the national order. The visitor can also show that poverty does not have to be dull; there is as much human interest in poor people who imaginatively tackle their condition as in affluent people painfully inventing ways to spend their wealth.

The ambassador who neglects these opportunities is doing a disservice to his country. When academics and savants from the developing world – not necessarily from his own country – are in the country of his posting for a while, he should not only keep in constant touch with them but help them to widen their contacts, as well as giving them the greater exposure that the diplomatic process makes possible. Thus the visitor should be enabled to meet important ministers and officials and key members of organizations involved in North–South relations and development. The embassy's senior diplomats can also discreetly pass on to the visitor those subtle signals within the host society that communicate tacitly, ignorance of which can lead to embarrassing mistakes. This is one of the great services an embassy offers to guests from home – a service of interpretation in more than just language, brought constantly up to date as mission personnel change and as the signals themselves change.

There is another function the members of an embassy can perform in relation to the universities of the developed world. That is to help harried bureaucrats from their own countries to enjoy in a university atmosphere a short, stimulating leave from the pressures of their offices. This will bring them up to date on their reading, and they can bring some of the day-to-day realities of Third-World government before the faculty and students among whom they are placed. Singapore does this extremely well, even to the point of having cabinet ministers go to Cambridge on minisabbaticals. The practice has incalculable results for the country and the individual on the one hand, and the university where he or she spends the time on the other. Most senior officials and cabinet ministers of developing countries are subject to pressures their counterparts in developed societies just cannot imagine. Unless they can at intervals, however short, remove themselves from the scene of their labours, they are in danger of running out of ideas or running out of steam due to sheer fatigue. If they take a three-month study break at a university in their own country it will be a break in name only. Their departments will be constantly consulting them for advice, and their opportunities for detached reflection will be desultory. The unfortunate official will have got the worst of two worlds: committed to reflection but unable to realize it; on leave from authority but constantly exercising it.

The importance of being miles from his own country, where his colleagues cease from troubling him and the telephone is at rest, lies in the perspective it gives and the focus it creates. It also serves to sharpen the official's capacity for conceptualization of what he or she is actually doing at home – placing the programmes within a broad context, so that function again becomes an aspect of strategy and strategy an aspect of long-term objectives. All this helps to prevent the disease from which most tired bureaucrats suffer – that of letting the parts gain at the expense of the whole. Finally, what such people offer to the universities where they spend their time is what the theologians call praxis – the marriage of theory and practice. This is good for both sides. The bureaucrat can hear criticisms without having to act the flinty protagonist for all that is done, and the academics will discover that the political absolutes to which so many of them are devoted are, in sober reality, not practical.

In addition, an ambassador and his staff have a special role with the students of his country at universities of the developed world. Not only is regular contact between the mission and those students critical, but the visits of embassy officials form an important contribution to their sense of identity in an alien environment. The ambassador and his staff become symbols of the students' national self-esteem. If he pays them regular visits, he strengthens their umbilical with the homeland – and of course he brings them up to date about its political, economic and cultural developments. The smaller and poorer the developing country, the more important the ambassador's presence to the students. On one level he represents the pride of sovereignty – a matter of great touchiness to the students, no matter how minute the country. On another level he represents not just his government's, but his society's, ongoing concern with their welfare, its interest in their achievements and its expectations of their return. He is a point of reference for them and a very important channel of communication both ways – from the government to them and from them to the government.

But apart from his symbolic and emotive role he has another from which many an ambassador might shrink. He stands *in loco parentis*, an important factor in many Third-World societies where there is great respect for the family elders and where it usually is assumed that authority connotes wisdom. Imagine the pride in a student's voice when he tells his fellows from the host society that he had lunch with his ambassador! It will go a long way toward deciding him either to return to his home country or, if this is not immediately feasible, to at least assist it from afar.

These functions are largely demanded by the reactions of Third-World students to the academic and cultural environment in which they find themselves. They are undergoing culture shock. They have come to the developed society to acquire skills, but they must relate to a whole environment that does not share their deepest assumptions, that does not understand their unspoken signals, that often expects of them patterns of behaviour with which they are not familiar. And meantime they are in a competitive atmosphere, where they are supposed to meet the expectations of those who sent them (parents or governments) as well as the demands of those who assess their academic competence. In short, they are called on to be at their best intellectually while trying to master a whole range of alien cultural norms. From this culture shock spring three reactions:

Some students become so assimilated that in outward behaviour, if not in colour, they become indistinguishable from the indigenes. They strive to become First Worlders, submerging the culture that they brought with them. They assume, rather outlandishly, the style, gestures, mannerisms and vocabulary of the milieu in which they find themselves, and this is particularly noticeable if the country in which they are studying has the same language as their own. What the outer forms of this assimilation indicate is the acquisition of assumptions normal to the inhabitants of the rich world – assumptions about material abundance, quick disposability, conspicuous waste and the right to comfort. Perhaps the most dangerous assumption is that advanced technology is normal and the absence of it back home renders life unbearable and professionalism impossible. This reaction stems from a sense that the backward are unworthy, that one's own culture is primitive or obscurantist, that salvation is to be found in imitation of the West and that those now at Western universities are the proper prophets of the new culture.

The reaction of others is the opposite – total rejection. Finding themselves estranged and discomfited, not a few Third-World students retreat into their own cultural cocoons and assume that their salvation lies in avoiding all corrupting contact with the host society – except in matters purely academic. They convince themselves that they have nothing to learn from the culture in which they are temporarily placed and affect a superiority of civilization, withdrawing themselves from any campus activity.

Sometimes they go over to the offensive and seek every occasion to proclaim the decadence of the host culture and the spiritual sanity, moral as well as political, of their own. The springs of this reaction lie also in the alienation created by culture shock. It seems to take too much emotional energy to learn the symbols, signals and hidden messages of the host culture, and the fear of becoming inauthentic, of losing one's identity, freezes their social attitudes. Understandably so, because the real fear is that of becoming a person of two worlds, at home in neither.

Where the campus has a sizeable contingent of students from the same part of the developing world, those who experience this second reaction may feel comfortable and secure. They have enough of their own kind with whom to make contact. Distancing themselves from the host culture does not condemn them to loneliness, and incestuousness becomes a virtue. But if their numbers are few, such a reaction can be painful, even harmful, to those involved, as they are without the protection of numbers or a variety of relationships. In either case this sort of reaction, like the first, is unhealthy for the individuals involved and denies them important learning experiences.

The third reaction is a critical curiosity about the host culture in which the students acquire some of its norms to conduct a dialogue with it. Motivated by a desire to penetrate rather than imitate, that sort of student sees the need not to reject, but to define. They encourage in themselves a sensitivity to the host culture, remembering that at some point in the future, when they have taken up positions of importance in their own country, they will have to meet and deal with at least some of the people encountered in the university or elsewhere in the host society.

Those who react in this way will engage in campus activities, joining societies and associations that interest them, developing acquaintances – even friendships – with students of the host country. They will also support or if necessary create associations of Third-World students, in which they can cement relationships with their fellows of other developing countries. Within those organizations they can examine more confidently the host society and bolster each other's self-assurance. Such a framework will not only help them to preserve their national identities, but also stimulate them to learn about the dynamics of international co-operation and the need for global perspective. They will have both a vehicle for debating their own concerns and an identifiable voice on campus. They may even produce a publication, through which they will learn, sometimes by judicious choice of argument and sometimes by injudicious mistakes, how to talk journalistically and therefore persuasively about the Third World to the First.

This of course is the healthiest of all reactions and one that Third-World ambassadors and their officers will wish to encourage. But encouragement means contact – not merely sending letters or bulletins but the solid contact of physical presence. If Third-World ambassadors visit universities for the purposes I have outlined earlier in this chapter, they can combine both purposes in one. They will spend time with the students from their own country as well as with the faculty and other interested students, not necessarily of their own country, who wish to discuss matters of global importance.

The diplomat should avoid the impression that spending time with his fellow-countrymen is a minor reason for his visit to a university. He and his officers should make a point of visiting universities with students from home, even where he or his staff have not been invited to speak to a larger audience. And when the ambassador visits his fellow-countrymen, he should go out of his way to host a campus event. This might be a reception or a cultural affair, to which he has invited not only the students he has come to see but assorted members of the faculty and administration, foreign-student advisers and leading students, particularly the executive members of internationally oriented societies.

In this way the ambassador or his deputy will help his countrymen and women, especially those who have just arrived, with contacts they can later explore for themselves. But on another level the senior diplomats will have a demonstration effect. Their behaviour will show how intelligently to cope with the host society while trying to get that society to take a more sensitive interest in foreign students.

Finally, of all people, students hunger for information from home. It is very satisfying for such students to have a newsletter put out by the mission specially for them – analytical, sophisticated, giving not just information but background, not just news but commentary – a total picture rather than segments of the show. Apart from giving the students something to get their teeth into, such a newsletter shows understanding of their concerns and sensitivity to their self-respect. Besides, it will stimulate the officers of the mission whose job it is to write and edit it, a desideratum whose fulfilment can be singularly lacking in small missions with bright junior staff hungering for something conceptual to do. In addition it will certainly be read not only by the students to whom it is addressed but by other students who want to make comparisons with what is happening elsewhere in the Third World.

Students away from home have an ambivalent attitude to embassy staffs. They respect the positions they hold, the things they do and the authority they represent. Often they are intensely critical of their persons, their lifestyles, their public musings, their convivial habits and even their interpretations of national policy. This is as natural as it is healthy. And no intelligent ambassador should feel wounded when these feelings are expressed. One way to make the positive side of the equation stronger than the negative is to keep the students informed, to stimulate them and to keep kindling the pride of their country, as well as rendering them intelligently knowledgeable about the strategies and tactics played out for international reconstruction.

6 Bread upon the Waters: Diplomats and Voluntary Associations

The sprouting of citizens' associations is seen in the societies of the West as a sign of national health. The wider their range, the more vital a society is assumed to be. Political parties and their many auxiliaries, naturally, give the polity its nature. But citizens are also involved in a broad network of clubs, societies and interest groups with widely varying purposes. These include pure pleasure, amateur or professional sport, personal enlightenment, communal enrichment, spiritual commitment, institutionalized benevolence, conservation (cultural, historical or naturalistic) as well as pressure groups.

The fundamentals of each nation's polity are sacralized in either a written or an unwritten constitution. But just as the interpretations of those fundamentals vary widely, so too do the groups representing the nuances of society – the variations in class, education, profession, conviction, calculation and vision. But all organized bodies wish to survive and to expand their ethos. This is why they all touch, some more obviously than others, the political order. That is why anyone who seeks to make sense of these societies must know something about these groups. Third-World diplomats cannot afford to ignore them, especially as the leverage of some is greater than their apparent lack of political affiliation suggests.

Heretofore, the altitude of an ambassador's contacts was the measure of his effectiveness. If he were on first-name terms with the men and women at the very top, nothing but good, it was assumed, could come of it for his country. In the decade of the 1980s, latitude has to be added to altitude.

Here a special grace – that of establishing relationships with people who do not make the critical decisions but without whose support those decisions cannot be made – is vital. The diplomat who is fitted only for the mountain-tops will be less than equipped for his advocacy of international change in the rich societies. For he is required to converse with, and to convince, people whose sturdy political sense is not covered by the dictionary definition of 'sophisticated', and whose qualifications for local influence do not include an alphabet of academic honours.

Obviously the ambassador and his staff will start with people who have an interest in a more equitable distribution of the world's resources. But if the diplomats allow themselves to be monopolized by such people they will be selling their case short. There are those who are not yet apprised of the gravity of the global situation and see only comforting distance between themselves and the developing world. They will have to be made more aware of the world's disturbing proximity; their awareness should be one of the major aims of ambassadors and their staffs.

Those who already show an initial interest in the state of the Third World often are people who are curious because they are uneasy – they simply want to know more for their own safety and survival. Sometimes the curiosity can degenerate into a callow hostility; sometimes it is sufficient to become scholarly analysis. There is the curiosity that grows into an informed solicitude; there is also the curiosity that matures into compassionate responsibility and action. And there are people in the rich societies concerned about the world because of deeply held philosophical or religious convictions. To this type the Third-World ambassador must pay special attention as the convictions take many forms, not the least significant being attempts to quicken the consciences of others.

Western societies are addicted to clubs, but of course the style of club life differs from country to country and from class to class. Among the upper echelons of British society, for instance, a club represents polished privacy – the concentration of men and sometimes of women who want to confirm their shared convictions without eroding their individuality. These clubs occasionally invite a speaker, but normally their members retreat to them to avoid having to listen. A Third-World ambassador should not expect these places to be receptive to the sort of speech common in the United Nations General Assembly. They may invite him to share their laconic fellowship and will tolerate his expressing opinions about the maldistribution of the world's resources *sotto voce*. But they will not forgive him for declamatory excellence. Here he will make his impact and perhaps his converts by the subtlety of clubmanship, not by the quality of his oratory.

But Britain is not unique in possessing these quiet retreats of privilege. Each Western country has them, and they prefer to be impermeable to missionaries and preachers. For they exist not to receive challenges to their convictions but to avoid them. That is not to say that a Third-World ambassador invited to join one (if he can afford it) should spurn the invitation. There may be in the club people of immense political leverage who have lived in a developing society and have acquired an affection for it. In this case the challenge is to turn receptiveness to the aspirations of one society into a desire for global equilibrium.

There are other types of club that exist because their members hunger for information and desire, as they like to say of themselves, to widen their horizons. Theirs is the cult of the exotic, of the unfamiliar; each feature presentation of another country amounts to a vicarious visit – not so much to learn as to look. Some of them meet only to have lunch and to hear 'entertaining speakers'. Others are service clubs doing valuable work in the local community, and occasionally further afield, whose main function in meeting is to foster togetherness. They have an itch to listen and a mature tolerance of the spoken word. If a speaker arouses their interest, there is no telling, given their commitment to service, where it will lead.

The information-seeking sort of club mentioned above consists, particularly in the English-speaking developed world, of various men's and women's institutes that make a whole culture out of their capacity to listen. They are frequently part of a national network, and a good speaker discovered in one branch can easily find himself or herself on the national circuit. They do not expect to be disturbed; they do expect to be amused. They may wish to increase their sense of wonder but not at the expense of their sense of security. In a word they are normally interested in variety but not in change. A diplomat who addresses them has to be particularly adroit. For he has to open their minds to new perceptions of the world without outraging their susceptibilities. Hence, a mastery of the art of making the unknown look more comforting than the known is indispensable to one engaged in altering the predilections of this kind of audience.

But there is a way of doing it. The speaker must first win their sympathy for those who suffer under the present international dispensations. He can then deftly point to the sort of dispensation that will reduce their suffering without diminishing the comfort of his hearers. These clubs are a heaven-sent opportunity, because their membership consists of people whom even an unusual diplomat is unlikely to meet anywhere else in his rounds – those described as the 'salt of the earth'. But clubs are also a peril for the wrong sort of speaker, for they cannot or will not digest heaviness; sentence and substance must be yeasted with wit and style. Because they are part of a national network, to lose one audience is often to lose all opportunities for making an impact.

When responding to invitations from women's clubs of this type, missions with female diplomats (and in the 1980s they should not be just a handful) will find them an incalculable asset if they are articulate. The upsurge of the feminist movement in North America and Western Europe has created a climate favourable to hearing about women in the developing countries. A woman diplomat talking about her country and its women to a women's club will establish areas of sympathy and, more important, bonds that no man can do. An adroit female who portrays the plight of Third-World women as largely an accentuation of the greater problems the Third World faces as a whole can make a decided impact on the thought processes of her audience. By establishing that the increasing equality with men of some women somewhere is made secure by the increasing equality of all women everywhere, a Third-World diplomat will provide what, in other spheres, is called linkage; she will help Third-World ideas to penetrate the First World to counter-balance the sort of penetration that the First World has been practising in the Third.

In fact the very presence of female diplomatic officers in Third-World missions in the rich societies has an eloquence all of its own. They give the lie to the assumption pervasive in Western countries that women play almost no intellectual and cultural part in the Third World, unless of course by that curious and singular concatenation of events that makes one of them a prime minister. There are difficulties, to be sure, in posting female foreign-service officers overseas, but at crucial times and in strategic places they are worth the difficulties their posting may pose.[13]

The service clubs, as they are called in North America but not in Europe, present a less delicately textured opportunity than those just mentioned, because of their nature, their objectives and the character of their membership. They exist to serve the community, and their service goes readily to the handicapped, the underprivileged, the aged, the infirm and those, particularly the young, in need of a palpable fraternity. Their network is international in the sense that they pervade the whole Western world and have chapters in many developing countries. They enjoy meeting at regional and international conferences, and there is close intercommunication between them.

They also have a tradition of concern that transcends national boundaries. Rotary in particular has a heritage of humanitarian work in every continent, with the richer clubs giving aid and even technical expertise to the poorer clubs in developing countries. Third-World ambassadors in North America are usually welcome speakers at Rotary, Kiwanis, Lions and Jaycees lunches and dinners. The same goes for their counterparts in Europe, particularly in Scandinavia and West Germany. Ambassadors are often expected to name projects that the chapters can adopt (as their terminology has it) in conjunction with counterpart clubs in the ambassador's country. Further, individual members of these clubs tend to take a human interest and not just a fiscal one in the overseas projects to which they have devoted themselves.

The members understand something about deprivation, inasmuch as these clubs exist to alleviate it or to create opportunities for escaping it. Individuals among them will have worked as consultants, bankers, business executives, volunteers or even sometimes as aid project officers in developing societies, thus acquiring first-hand knowledge of the constraints under which governments and people operate. True, the deprivation they are normally exposed to is that in their own societies, which bears little comparison to the misery of the millions in poor countries. But they have characteristics that give an ambassador from the developing world an entrée into their minds and sympathies.

First, they are disturbed that some cannot use opportunities theoretically available to all. According to their philosophy, where handicap is permanent they must seek to alleviate it; where it is not they must seek to remove it. They will heed an approach to development that takes equality of opportunity as its starting point, because with them that is an article of faith. An ambassador should be able to show them that what developing countries

really want is precisely that on which they base their own conceptions of a just society. This approach will give them something
to ponder.

Second, their ideals are international even though their activity
is primarily local. They see the world as a unity – although
tending to exclude those areas described as socialist – and they
should be willing to follow an ambassador who subtly demonstrates that disparity is the most potent destroyer of unity.

Third, their aim is stability within societies as well as in the
relations between them; their devotion is to an orderly world. The
ambassador can show that where there is no justice in distribution
there can be no order or equilibrium. Their own postulates thus
lead persuasively to the same conclusions that otherwise greatly
alarm them when they hear them proclaimed in the polemics of
the United Nations General Assembly.

The dignity of man is one of the tenets of these clubs. It is a
tenet a Third-World ambassador shares. Charity, he will
emphasize, however high-minded, in some ways diminishes both
the giver and the receiver, for it reminds the recipient of help-
lessness and the donor of guilt. All agree it is no substitute for
justice. Nor, the diplomat will add, is aid – which, like charity, is
a symptom of a world that has no balance. Better a more
balanced international order and little aid than massive aid (not
forthcoming anyway) and an unbalanced international order.
Human dignity, the diplomat will demonstrate, is substantially
assured when people are empowered to produce for a market that
rewards them with growing incentives to produce more. Human
dignity is eroded when a market renders people so enfeebled that
they are reduced to despairing mendicants. As a gloss of this
theme, the diplomat will spotlight a truth his audiences will be
delighted to affirm: productive people have independence of
spirit, which gives them pride in their production, and a grasp of
the interdependence of mankind, which gives them faith in
exchange. That is both good business and sound morality, the
application of which should not be limited to a fraction of the
world's population. He will then climax his argument by showing
that the proposals for the NIEO and its ancillaries promote
human dignity globally, on the assumption that a balance of
dignities is better for peace than a balance of deterrents.

But I cannot too heavily emphasize that when diplomats
converse with service clubs the *human* element must be

paramount. What will wake up economists and politicians – the statistics, the abstractions and the manoeuvrings of states – will send club members to sleep.

Obviously no spokesman for the Third World can discuss human dignity without dealing with the economics and politics on which that dignity so heavily depends. But it should be done by interweaving the day-to-day grind of poverty with the abstractions, by showing how the demands of the rich negate the assiduity of the poor. To do this well, diplomats need to pool not only their understanding of these clubs but also their techniques of selection and illustration that make presentations effective.

He or she who addresses a service club must be prepared for sharp questioning. Multinational corporations encourage their members to join such clubs to demonstrate their concern for the communities in which they operate. It is not just a preference, it is a policy. Such people are often the leaders in projects directed to help developing countries. They are consequently bound to place a high value on compassion, which leads to aid for the sufferers but not to any changes in the condition that renders their suffering inevitable. These persons will certainly argue the identity of interest between their corporate employers and the countries where they operate. A diplomat who presents the case for change in the present global economic structure must expect the arguments against him to be informed, incisive and statistically precise.

The service clubs provide the diplomat not only with a platform but an access to the local media. Addresses by ambassadors or their senior officers to Rotarians, Kiwanis, Jaycees and similar clubs are usually given some coverage, if not on the radio at least in one of the daily papers, and an address may even earn editorial notice. There are two reasons for this. First, as ambassadors tend to stay close to the capital, a visit to a more distant city becomes enough of a local event for the media to take notice. Second, there is usually one journalist, often more, who belongs to the club and is willing to write a story of the ambassador's visit.[14] And if the presentation is sufficiently noteworthy the diplomat will find himself invited to elaborate on radio or television. These opportunities should not be ignored or sidetracked by representatives of developing countries. Apart from the obvious advantages of media exposure, they can lead to requests from concerned individuals for further information, or from concerned groups for documentation. Contacts so made should be maintained and developed by the mission.

Listening and service clubs do not exhaust the list of associations that enable an ambassador and his staff to broaden the scope of their representations. Every Western society has specialized, internationally oriented, research institutes devoted to comparative analysis. Some of these bodies deal with economic trends, some with the development of technology; others are public policy institutes examining the behaviour of governments in rich and poor societies. Frequently there are geographic societies with concerns wider than their title suggests, and inevitably there are institutes of international affairs. Medical societies are part of the staple of First-World existence. Some look only to their own concerns; others have members who have travelled or served in developing countries, frequently as advisers, and want to maintain their contacts.

No one ambassador or mission can adequately relate to all these groups even some of the time, but not to relate to some of them most of the time would be a grave disservice to the country represented and to the cause of the developing world as a whole. What is important is to make a careful selection of those with whom the embassy should maintain relationships, rather than leaving this process to an impulsive adhocracy. Appropriate contacts, such as are often made at receptions or dinners, should be followed up by regular written communications. Selection will obviously be based on a country's current priorities and on the receptivity of the particular organization to development issues. The ambassador and his staff will aim to interest members of some groups that, even though they show no initial concern for the Third World, have the prestige and influence in their own communities to spread their concern, once awakened, to others.

Here the combination of personal contact and supply of *suitable* written material is critical. Without the personal spark, there may be no kindling of interest; without the sustenance of reading material there will certainly be no maturing of a relationship. When the diplomat has created in key members of an organization an openness to what his country is saying and doing, the second stage becomes as important as the first. The mission's duty is then to supply not propaganda, which can easily be recognized, but positional documents, selections from recent monographs, background papers presented at conferences or to committees of UN organizations – relevant distillations of thought, scholarship and praxis published in the home country and elsewhere.

Documentation is good; putting those interested in touch with the authors of the documents is even better. The relationship will then take on a momentum of its own, which is precisely the point of initiating it. When this happens, it is important that the mission be kept informed through the ministry of foreign affairs of developments. Such connections sometimes lead to an interest so active that the organization forms, at its own suggestion or otherwise, a relationship with its opposite number in the developing country. This can go to the extent of supplying expertise or consultants for projects, financed by an international organization or an aid agency of the country to which the mission is accredited. This is particularly likely to be the case with medical, engineering and technological groups, although it also happens with other types of organizations.

One of the prime functions of an embassy is to bring together people with similar skills in the country of origin and in the country of posting. Government officials and advisers form the international jet-set these days, a stationary bureaucrat being, like a stationary eagle, a contradiction in terms. But when the officials arrive in a developed country as part of a delegation, they tend to meet only their opposite numbers in government. Here is the justification for a well-planned diplomatic reception. An ambassador with his eye to the future and his ear to the ground will invite some members of professional associations to meet his officials. He and his staff must be careful first to brief his visitors on the importance of links with these people, then to ensure contact is made. The increase in personal relationships will contribute to an increase in warmth and understanding between the two societies – a truism that should not need to be stated but is in fact often overlooked. The contacts will ensure that sympathetic and sensitive professionals in developed societies will influence the perceptions of development of their colleagues in their own countries. This will be the more convincing because it is not done through official channels or by the paid servants of the state. It can mean that suspicion will give way to critical sympathy; more fundamentally, indifference will be exchanged for thoughtful concern.

With the international affairs institutes, an ambassador's relations will necessarily be in the form of dialogue. Here his special task is to disabuse the membership of misconceptions both about the functioning of Third-World countries and the nature of Third-World proposals. It does not need much elaboration these days to point out that developing countries are the victims of considerable stereotyping in the rich societies – a stereotyping as pervasive as it is pernicious. What is surprising is that such stereotyping prevails at levels where the impact of university education, foreign travel and intellectual discourse would lead one not to expect it. There is a widespread assumption of corruption, inefficiency, lethargy and hot-headedness, but there is also a curious lack of appreciation of why the Third World is seriously attempting to organize itself.

The self-contradiction displayed on this last point is as old as it is impolitic. When the developing countries do not concert their actions they are rebuked by the pundits of developed societies for a lack of political will. But when they do organize themselves, the Third World is condemned for its bellicose intentions. This smacks of the attitudes of the English upper classes in the nineteenth century toward the attempts of working-class people to improve their condition: they were dismissed as men of straw when cohesion was lacking, but branded as rabid revolutionaries when their cohesion was proven.

The members of the international affairs institutes and clubs read both the sophisticated material put out by the organizations themselves and the journals dealing with world affairs. But the great majority of them see things almost exclusively in First-World perspectives. They may be concerned with better standards of living in developing countries, but the prescriptions they offer are based on 'what is good for the West is good for the rest' – a maxim that supports the *status quo*. Change, when it comes, must be remedial, not structural. For they associate the economic and political health of the world with the intellectual and political primacy of the West, and the systems of the world with the systems of the West.

Their virtue is that they will listen to a point of view different from their own. Their value to a Third-World ambassador lies in the two functions they perform: they offer prudent options to those who formulate foreign policy, and they involve their membership in a sustained analysis of international trends. Accordingly, they will consider the effects of change on their stability. And they will frequently countenance reform, because updating the system strengthens its foundations. Awareness is their method, survival of the familiar their aim. This is the starting point of a Third-World diplomat's dialogue with them. Although their reading may be wide, their understanding of the Third World is often slim. The job of the diplomat is to direct their reading to the substantial contributions to the dialogue on economic and structural change made by Third-World thinkers and some of their own most distinguished writers.

Their information on the Third World is, after all, often so selective as to be sectarian. They learn of rhetoric unmatched by realism, of aid misused and of a preference for prestige projects over productive ones in developing countries. They are seldom told of major creative experiments, or of the hard work and imaginative ingenuity that groups and even governments in developing societies bring to the solution of their problems. Most disturbing of all, they often harbour thoughts about the United Nations that deny it legitimacy or utility. They are led to see it as a vast vaudeville, of the powerless trying to change the settled order of things by the only potency they are presumed to possess – words. They perceive the spokesmen of developing nations as 'mythologians' – people who pass resolutions in the General Assembly in the hope of creating a myth that will eventually become familiar enough to be accepted as fact. Many of them deride the UN as a failure because the poor have a majority that the powerful can override. They contend its strongest characteristic is absurd posturing and its achievements are tiny. Finally, there are some who see the UN as a cathartic safety-valve for the resentments of the indigent against the affluent.

To counter these attitudes, ambassadors from the Third World need to agree among themselves on the kinds of argument that will put the issue into proper perspective. Together they can form a consensus on their fundamental propositions for change while still accepting that there are differences of emphasis or method between one group of countries and another. The persuasiveness of what they say will depend on its scope. Their case must be based not on the needs of any one country, but it may be illuminated by the case of each country and by the solid underpinning of the case, the absence of moralizing and the evidence of practical programme.

If associations are not approached collectively, it is likely they will cling to the *status quo*. The collective advocacy will best serve when the listeners are able to compare the individual presentations. The presentations will all point to the same conclusions or they will adumbrate proposals the speakers have agreed on. But they do not necessarily have to be replicas of each other in style or approach. What the speakers will be after is the highest common factor not the lowest common denominator.

The exercise of concerting positions for presentation and of working out consensus will relieve many a diplomatic day from the tedium of routine. It is a rigorous exercise, unquestionably, but it can also be wonderfully concentrating. It will endow bilateral diplomacy with something of the stimulation of multilateral diplomacy without the hothouse atmosphere. A collective approach implies disciplined thought, and the experience gained in it will prepare Third-World diplomats for the age of collective negotiations.

The effect of all this will be cumulative rather than immediate, and pervasive before it becomes implanted. The Third World, responding in unity and with lucidity and subtlety to criticisms and questions, will deserve at least attention and at best consideration. This unity, if presented with discretion, careful consideration of the context and sensitive use of acceptable symbols, can remove the fears of thinking people in the rich countries over what they see as the menace of Third-World cohesion. Properly portrayed, unity indicates not a ganging up (which since 1973 has been the persistent nightmare among the rich), but a getting together – for purposes that are creative rather than aggressive. In the increasingly popular idiom in Britain, the USA, West Germany and Canada, the Third World is now activating a philosophy of self-help. As the rich countries would themselves say, independent survival is better than aided survival.

In particular, Third-World ambassadors will have to point, by inference rather than directly, to the dangers inherent in the Western drift to protectionism. The temptation to erect high tariff walls is strong in Europe and the United States. Protectionism is, in the eyes of many sober analysts, less a boosting mechanism than a policy of anxiety disguised as certitude – nationalism gone sulky in an age when nationalism should be treading generously. There is also a belief that when developing countries protest against protectionism they are purely self-serving; they expect to accelerate their own development at the expense of the developed countries in a heads-I-win, tails-you-lose type of manoeuvre. Some of those most thoughtful in the West are telling their fellows that the constraints they are now experiencing signal the end of a period of exuberant growth, that the age of soaring economies must be followed by the age of sharing economies, that the earth's resources have to be husbanded rather than exploited and that the husbandry must be global rather than sectoral. Representatives of the Third World must make full use of these thinkers.

Insecurity is frequently the mother of invention. What men will not recognize in a period of stability they recognize in apprehension. This phenomenon can lead to a reappraisal of conventional wisdom, if it is well handled. It is to the promotion of alternatives that Third-World ambassadors and their missions must turn. The case against protectionism has to be made not only at the level of the UN and its agencies; it also has to be made in the constituencies of Western political leaders and trade unionists. In fact, a dialogue on the matter has to be carried on within the rich nations as well as between the rich and the poor ones.

Third-World ambassadors must devote their energies to strengthening the voices of innovation. The necessarily technical reports produced by experts on the subject must be made more palatable and persuasive. The ambassadors must make themselves and their knowledgeable staff more available for consultation. Most important, they must establish among themselves a pool of documentation, constantly augmented by all the missions, available to those wishing to learn more about the many aspects of the Third-World case. The material made available must be carefully vetted. Polemics will drive away the thoughtful. Carefully researched material will encourage the analytical. A lucid, calm reasonableness, which unemotionally explains the probable consequences of Western disengagement, will attract readers. Ivan Head, President of the International Development Research Centre in Ottawa, has said, 'Injustice along the North–South axis of the international community is more a product of indifference than of greed, more of inertia and ignorance than intention.'[15] This implies that an ambassador's aim is the extension of consciousness, an extension best achieved by appeals to enlightened self-interest rather than a vitriolic condemnation of selfishness.

There is no question that this involves a lot of work. But the workload can be lightened and enlivened by sensitive and adroit co-operation among the missions of the Third World. Young embassy officials, thirsting after grander things than daily routine, will respond eagerly to this sort of challenge. These officers already meet at cocktails, but they tend to divide into regional groups, particularly in capitals where there are many missions. Their occasional sorties into other groups are marginal and not very meaningful. But the Third World is more than the sum of its regional parts. There is no better way for a junior officer to learn this than by working with his Third-World colleagues in sifting, assessing and collating material for the campaign for a more just world. Such activity will engender cohesiveness. It will transfer a young officer's resolve into a habit. As he is promoted he will take upward a greater vision of development and a commitment to collective action matured by his experience.

It should not be forgotten that a mission, besides being a functioning unit, has a purpose as an educational experience for its junior members. If in their early postings these young people learn certain behaviours, they may find it difficult to shed them later. Thus it is for them an indispensable experience to learn the difference between what can be done collectively by embassies and what should be reserved for purely national operations.

Promoting co-operation is a creative but demanding activity, and it is not easily learned in the current practice of diplomacy. The guidelines that inform that practice remain based, alas, on the old dogmas of the nation-state.

So far I have been talking about preaching to the unconverted. But the converted exist in every Western society – not, to be sure, in large numbers or necessarily well organized or always fully understanding the principles of what they believe in. But they exist. And they frequently look to embassies of developing countries for the waters of life, and are as frequently drowned in a cascade of clichés. Or where they seek advice, they are often given a drink instead. Coctails can often be a convivial pat on the head that confirms the rightness of their cause but does nothing to help define their strategies.

The converted tend to leave ambassadors and their officers to the preoccupations of embassy work, getting their material direct from agencies within Third-World countries or the United Nations and making their case without the assistance of diplomats. As Dr Samuel Johnson might have observed, 'Is not an ambassador one who looks with unconcern on a man struggling for life in the water and when he has reached the ground encounters him with help?' Third-World missions should encourage and assist, within a reasonable discretion, these individuals and groups.

An embassy officially and its officers personally will not make or maintain contact with groups whose aim is the overthrow of the state by violent means. This prohibition is totally *de rigueur*. Likewise, diplomatic contact with those who call for a better distribution of the earth's resources by a withering away of the state is counterproductive for an embassy's credibility. The lunatic or utopian fringes are not grist for any ambassador's mill. It may be interesting to know something about them; it is not prudent to know them – if only because their company will alienate those who are likely to wield influence where it counts.

But there are in Western societies groups more within the mainstreams of life who are alive to the dangers of the world as it is, as well as to the possibilities of the world as it could be. They see the problem as one of perception, yet they know that perception without political will is faith without works. Let us look at what these groups are and what sort of people comprise them.

First, there are the environmentalists and the ecologists, people overwhelmingly conscious of the fragility and the finitude of the earth. They see around them untold exploitation, amounting almost to rape, of the world's resources by mindless consumerism. Their concern for the future is as acute as their devotion to the present; they want to ensure that the future world will be habitable by making those who live in the present world aware of their dangerously foreclosing behaviour. They worry primarily about the whole world; by inference they also worry about the developing world. Their moral passion is for creative moderation in the use of world resources, for sound ecological commonsense.

Then there are those who believe in the oneness of the world and the unity of man. Their case subsumes much of what the Third World is saying. They counsel against using up too much too soon, which is an admonition to that one-eighth of the world's people that consumes more than four-fifths of its resources. They preach moderation, which is only practical with equitable distribution and the increasing use of renewable resources. Their message is that developed and developing countries must exercise the political will necessary to prevent exhaustion of the earth's resources by those non-territorial octopuses, the transnational corporations. They see two processes that threaten the earth's future: the erosion of immense areas of soil when the poor are driven, for want of fuel, to cut down the trees in their vicinity, and the prodigal depletion of the earth's non-renewable resources by waste of fossil fuels. Both these processes, they say, will irreparably destroy the oneness of the earth. And when the balance of the ecology is destroyed, what is the relevance of that dearly beloved (by the politicians) other balance, the balance of payments?

With these groups, diplomats from the Third World can have valuable relations. For very substantial reasons. First, they are part of the conscience of the West. They are a counterculture that opposes not only the establishment, but the values that place a premium on the present at the expense of the future, the values that hold that enough is never enough. Second, their members include some of the most creative minds in the West – academics who transcend their disciplines, writers who tremble for the world, thinkers (like the late Barbara Ward) whose minds range over more than one province of knowledge, students who refuse to limit their concerns, and ordinary citizens who for whatever reason eschew the race to keep up with the Joneses and resolve only to keep themselves in good health. Third, these ideas have already become part of the mental bag and baggage of significant minorities in the developed world. Pressure groups have been formed to restore the earth's beauty after the extraction of ores. Animal sanctuaries are becoming larger and more respected. The battle against pollution has been joined. The recycling of waste, particularly in Scandinavia, has become normal.

What a Third-World ambassador must do is to bring all this together and make it into something larger. The emphasis is right, but the individual views are restricted. He has to widen their scope. He must make people understand that immense poverty is a menace not just to the physical environment, but also to the globe's continuing peaceful existence. He must explain that deforestation is only one of many destructive results of poverty and that poor people, pressed by their own numbers, have no taste for conservation either of the ecology around them or the international polity over them. Those who believe in the oneness of the earth, who have a commitment to the future, should broaden their campaign to include a better deal for the wretched of the earth. For as long as they are crushed, the only interest in the future these people can have is that of getting through the day ahead of them.

These groups will have made their own analysis of the malign effect on their environment of the extractive philosophy of the wealthy. The Third-World diplomat will add to that his own analysis of the equally malign effects on developing societies of being undernourished tributaries to the river of affluence. He will explain that in many poor societies food is produced for the tables of the rich countries while all but a fragment of the population go undernourished. That while a few become glutted, millions become gutted, and there is a direct causal relationship between the two states.

But the greatest contribution an ambassador can make is the idea of 'food first'. Enabling the hungry of the earth to feed themselves, encouraging the privileged to desist from over-feeding, returning fecundity to the earth through intelligent agriculture, making survival with security possible for the millions and thereby enabling the millions to restrict their numbers – this interconnection of cause and effect hinges on the most fundamental factor, food. This is the point of departure for a Third-World ambassador trying to focus concern on first, the health of the earth and second, a moderation in the increase in numbers of its people.

One of the most potent forces by which the Western mind becomes conscious of the injustice in the prevailing structures is the church. No Third-World ambassador can therefore afford to ignore the role of the churches. But few Third-World ambassadors, unless they are practising Christians, understand the churches well enough to work with them. Some ambassadors positively fear the churches; others simply ignore them. But churches are, or ought to be, among a Third-World ambassador's strongest allies.

The churches are the most organized and structured embodiment of the conscience of the West. They have a long and intimate relationship with the Western mind – because they helped shape it – even when that mind has gone secular. And they are as complex as the mind they shaped. Recognition of the potential of the churches and an understanding of their actuality are crucial for Third-World envoys.

If we look at the signals closely we will make a number of significant discoveries. The first is that many of the churches are in the middle of a stocktaking process. They are examining their record in relation to what are now known as developing countries. The soul-searching has sparked a fierce debate between two schools of thought – those who believe that the missionary movement of the eighteenth, nineteenth and twentieth centuries was right in motivation and methods, and those who feel that the churches were as much colonizers as the proconsuls and the merchants and have more to atone for. Those who espouse the first view feel by and large that the Third World still needs the example, if not the leadership, of the First. Capitalism, as they see it, makes for the best of all possible worlds, and the churches exist to purify the ethos of free enterprise, to soften its more abrasive features, and to restore to vigour and community those bruised by it. Socialism they see as destructive both of the soul and of the society; it is wrong because it goes against the sovereignty of God, because it belongs to a family of concepts born of atheism out of social anger and because it does not bear the stamp of Euro-America.

I said *by and large*, for while these religious and secular convictions are the mark of the fundamentalist, there are small but significant numbers of theologically conservative Christians with more radical views of development and a grasp of Third-World realities. An ambassador who sees all conservative churchmen as economic fundamentalists would be guilty not only of great oversimplification, but also of ignoring groups of articulate allies. Ronald J. Sider's book *Rich Christians in an Age of Hunger*[16] exposes the myth that there is an unvarying connection between theological conservatism and economic conservatism. Fiercely disputed in Western societies, it is one of the most trenchant criticisms of the international economic *status quo* to come from the pen of an American Christian. It cogently illustrates the case for an NIEO.

The revisionists in the Western Christian world are more repentant of the past and devoted to a changed future. They know their churches have often given unction to injustice and blessed with conviction what proved to be (for them) structurally convenient. They are not given to righteous irritation when developing world spokesmen accuse the churches of past and sometimes continuing collaboration with 'imperialism' (classical or neo-). They understand the charge, accept some of the analysis and commit their energies to the struggle for a more humane and just world order.

Most of them are liberal churchmen, as concerned that their faith should speak to people as that people should speak to their faith. They are not averse to finding the inspiration of the Holy Spirit in the movements for justice and liberation, and their devotion is to equality of opportunity for all the world's peoples. Their faith leads them to be critical of concentrations of wealth amid massive poverty, and they are committed to the eradication both of suffering and the structures that produce it.

They do not propose socialism as the only road to healthy national societies, yet they are not categorically opposed to it. If it preserves fundamental human rights (in their reckoning freedom of speech, movement and dissent) and allows for the changing of governments by free and fair elections (or, in one-party states, the changing of personnel within governments by the same process), they will grant that socialism may be a lever of development. They may even go further. If a socialist state generates in its people the drive and resourcefulness to create wealth and equitably distribute it, they will support it as an adequate, relevant instrument for liberation from poverty.

To them, justice in distribution and freedom of expression are human rights of equal standing. So they see in some socialist states a failure to allow true liberation to take place, and they see in some capitalist states a failure to correct cruel economic imbalances by the state's refusal to intervene in the process of distribution. What they require, then, in political structures is an equilibrium between the freedoms they hold dear and the development they deem necessary. By the imperatives of their mission they are universalists, not cultural chauvinists. They are not so devoted to their present environment that they assume it is the only legitimate one. But they believe that the shrinkage of the globe, by modern communications and the growth of population, has turned the ethical demands of Christianity from an obedience that makes men good into the sole condition that makes man possible. In short, they maintain that the ten commandments of the Old Testament and the two commandments of the New are now the groundrules for human survival.

There is yet another school of thought in the West. It is smaller than the liberal middle and less strident than the conservative right, but it is articulate, highly analytic and politically oriented – the Christian left. Its adherents are usually socialist but not dogmatically so. Their analysis of underdevelopment they take from Marx, but they do not equate hate with hope. Nor do they believe that the future of man is scientifically determined – rather it is man under God who is the agent of historical change; choice, not inevitability, is the driving force.

As they see the world there are oppressors and oppressed, the oppressed being the poor of the Third World and the oppressors being the rich nations. Capitalism, frequently the enterprises of Third-World elites that are locally interdependent with the multinational corporations, is in their reckoning the fundamental cause of poverty in Latin America, Africa and southeast Asia. This can only be remedied by changes in the power structure in all developing societies, by revolution if necessary but not necessarily by revolution. God, in their theology, is the God of the poor and it is the poor who must make the changes. This will be brought about when the poor become conscious that social structures are not immutable. What some men have made other men can change if they have the conviction that there is a more just alternative. The liberation of the oppressed, this school maintains, must be accompanied by the liberation of the oppressors. The one will be achieved by radical structural changes in the developing countries and the other by radical changes of perception in the rich countries.

Basic to their belief is the conviction that millions of ordinary citizens in Western industrialized societies are unwittingly participants in and beneficiaries from the system that keeps millions of their fellow men below the bread line. The rich must therefore be consciencized as much as the poor, which may surprise many who think that that particular process is designed only for the deprived. Both the liberal middle and the radical left emphasize the need for structural change, not only within the societies of the First and Third Worlds, but in the international order as well. Further, they not only accept the necessity for new international as well as local orders; they are committed to helping create them. As a prelude they are prepared – in fact they have already begun – to bring before their own constituencies the case for restructuring the global order.

This is not always easy. Many who attend churches in the rich societies are looking for the comfortable pew. Particularly in the United States and West Germany, people do not go to church to review the social fabric or to observe its inadequacies but, in the togetherness of prayer, to uphold it. Those church leaders, lay and clerical, with a global vision and some understanding of the need for change have to be courageous and skilful in putting forward plans for an alternative world.

Part of the skill in showing the relationship between the Christian ethic and the need for change lies in a good grasp not of just what is needed but of what is involved. The objectives of change are one thing, the methodology of change is another. Here the church leaders, unless they are themselves economists or political scientists, need continuing expert advice.

It is at this point that the co-operation between Third-World diplomats and churchmen becomes vital. Both sides have to be aware not only of what is needed, but of concrete proposals for international reconstruction. Without the awareness there will be no search for a programme; without a programme awareness will remain pietistic. But first it will be necessary to induce attitudes receptive to change among the laypeople, of whom some may be nationally prominent, others locally prominent and many ordinary, but active citizens.

Providentially, concerns common to diplomats and churchmen have recently become important and fundamental. A brief look at the most significant ones is useful here.

First, the churches are committed to a world of greater justice.[17] Third-World diplomats are concerned with a more equitable and efficacious distribution of the globe's material resources. That justice in distribution makes for a healthier international economy can lead to a careful study of such proposals as commodity stabilization and price indexation, which will assist developing countries increase their food production.

Second, Christians are increasingly concerned with power and the abuse of it; manipulation of the many by the few is steadily becoming the target of their moral indignation. Diplomats are deeply aware that the world marketing system is a prime example of concentrated power and unabashed manipulation. Case studies of Third-World countries that are obvious victims of such abuse of power should be made available to church study groups. Detail should be enough to drive home the lessons and spell out the human implications, besides making the point that the system is beginning to work against its erstwhile beneficiaries. The church groups thus will see its diminishing efficiency as well as its lack of morality.

Third, waste and overindulgence are both contrary to the Christian ethic. The fact that both activities are a philosophy of life in the rich societies is, for churchmen, evidence of a far departure from spiritual values. For the Third-World poor it represents a far departure from a sense of balance in the habitation of the earth. Here churchmen and diplomats can co-operate to show the sapping effects on the health of those who live by indulgence. Numerous studies are available on this subject. The diplomat can also use the great reports published by the World Health Organization, Food and Agriculture Organization and other international bodies, which document the inevitable depletion of the earth's resources if the present way of using them continues unabated. Extraction then becomes as much a moral as a technologic issue, and laypeople will see the common ground between their faith and international economic activities.

Fourth, children occupy a central place in Christian thought and feeling. Their fate and their future are of burning concern to the great majority of congregations. To demonstrate, as any diplomat can readily do, the miseries of millions of children in developing countries and the hopelessness with which their lives are smitten is to touch a very responsive chord among Christians in developed societies. Those who seek a world of less violence and greater reasonableness see the importance of the quality of children's lives; to them the economic realities that render children destitute assume a moral dimension that makes indifference intolerable.

Fifth, Christians believe that choice is destiny and that the human will (under God) is the fashioner of history. Increasingly they recognize that important choices can seldom be apolitical, than non-involvement in the causes of their day is not a Christian option and that the exercise of the will must not be left only to governments.[18] Convinced that ordinary citizens can make big changes and force their governments to go along with them, they are more ready now than twenty years ago to have a share in shaping the future. Ethics and politics, for them, are not mutually exclusive domains. The ordering of the world as Christians want it is a moral ordering, and a new approach to economics is an instrument to this end. The Brandt Report,[19]

Interfutures,[20] *The Global 2000 Report,*[21] the *World Develop-ment Report 1980*,[22] all in different languages say the same thing. When churchmen and diplomats assist each other to spread word of these reports, they are taking part in an awakening process.

Churches, one need hardly add, are frequently potent pressure groups, once their targets are identified and their strategies carefully formulated. One has only to look at the campaign by members of some denominations in North America against banks that deal in South Africa and did in Rhodesia before it became Zimbabwe. The campaign embarrassed the banks. The shock-wave it caused around Christendom led a number of people, not all Christian, to re-examine their involvement in these places. The controversial decision of the World Council of Churches to contribute funds for the health and education of the freedom fighters who eventually brought down Ian Smith's regime was first attacked by many middle-of-the-road churchmen, then allowed to stand as legitimate, particularly when it was seen how smooth was the transition to an independent Zimbabwe under the government of Robert Mugabe.

But the churches, at least their liberal and radical wings, do more than create a constituency favourable to change; they also take part directly in development. And this in three distinct forms.

First, they often relay considerable sums of money to churches in developing countries for developmental projects. In fact a number of church leaders in the developed countries would rather send aid for this purpose than for the more traditional object of maintaining church buildings or recruiting new members. Where a local church (or, better, a set of local churches) undertakes to render a community service that confers needed skills or induces self-reliance, churches in Europe and North America respond eagerly and with hard cash. A tacit maxim seems to guide their response: the smaller the church, the more it will be assisted if its projects are clearly developmental. It may surprise not a few diplomats that many developing world churches provide service out of all proportion to their numerical or financial weight. Ambassadors who are interested and whose governments do not officially discourage church contributions to national growth can sometimes help to bring together concerned church people in rich countries and the churches in their own countries who are so engaged.

Second, some large churches undertake schemes in developing

societies without input from the local churches. They see a need, allocate resources, hire and pay skilled people and sometimes deal directly with governments in the pursuit of their service. This is not proselytism or missionary work in the strictly clerical sense – their aim is not to convert souls but to convert that which is barren to fecund production. A Third-World ambassador who tries suspiciously to thwart these good works will do considerable disservice to the cause of development as a whole and his own country in particular. (Unless of course his government has an ideology that disapproves of all churches or is a theocracy of a different religion.) His business is to examine the feasibility of the project, its relevance to his society's objectives and the motive that inspires it. Once he is satisfied that there is no concealed political objective, such as confirming Western norms, he should encourage and assist the scheme.

And if a pure concern for human welfare is the motive, its benefits are likely to be twofold: better health and self-reliance among those helped and better understanding of development among those who carry out the project. Television gives the people of the rich countries a one-dimensional view of poverty. Actual involvement in a project will show participants its causes and teach them critically to assess ways of change. An ambassador who promotes such co-operation is helping to create exactly what the developing world needs – a constituency of people in the rich societies who have made contact with the victims of an unjust system and who are thereby motivated to work hard and intelligently for a just one.

Third, the experts, consultants and skilled personnel that the churches hire and pay are generally less expensive than those a government provides or those from the great secular international organizations. But they are not less effective. In fact they often offer far more value than the money they are paid. In addition their service is less likely to carry ideological overtones than that offered by consultants dispatched by governments of developed countries or those from transnational corporations. Their lifestyle is also nearer to that of the people they work among, and they often go beyond the call of duty, providing services with humanity, warmth and skill. For all these reasons, Third-World diplomats should learn what is going on with the churches I have described as liberal, radical or even theologically conservative but developmentally radical.

A great opportunity offers itself to diplomats from the developing world whenever international games take place in the developed countries where they are posted. Sport permeates all spheres of national life, stimulating a large desire to find out something about 'the other side' or the nations from which the contestants come. It attracts the young in search of physical specimens to admire, and it attracts the mature in search of excitement and non-lethal aggression. The cult of skill and strategy appeals to all ages.

That is why it offers this opportunity to ambassadors from the developing world to raise the consciousness of the rich societies about their own. The Commonwealth Games provide a good example, but the lessons are of wider application. Whenever they are held in a developed Commonwealth country, missions whose countries are sending teams are bombarded with requests for material – not only on the teams, but on the countries and their culture. The requests come in many forms: those running the games seek information on the geography, economics, religions and culture of the contributing countries. The media require visual material or background films and even scholarly works on aspects of those societies. Amateur sport associations ask for biodata on the star performers. There is a universal demand for national flags, national symbols, coats of arms, buttons and of course explanations of what these mean. Even stamps are in demand from schoolchildren and philatelists.

Schools grow acutely hungry for material to be used in their classrooms. Teachers exploit this opportunity to stimulate among their students an interest in the geography, sociology, economics and culture of the participating countries. Frequently many young people first learn where a developing country is during the run-up to the games. Nothing like sport contributes so sharply to a rise in geographical awareness.

What is true of the Commonwealth Games is true of continental games and, on a global scale, of the Olympics, as well as of such single-feature events as the World Cup. All these sporting occasions present distinct opportunities: to seize them Third-World diplomats have to be energetic and well prepared.

But if a lot depends on the missions, even more depends on the home governments, who determine strategy while the missions carry out the tactics. No developing country can respond to all the queries it receives. Accordingly, there has to be a selection of aims, a carefully worked out concept of what images it wants to create through the opportunity of the games.

On the advice of its mission, the government of a developing country must decide where the most telling and enduring impact can be made. It will then shape its material in the light of that decision. For instance, a government might conclude that the most effective way to instruct the host country is through stamps. So it will allocate some of its scarce resources to new issues that amateurs and professionals will want to collect.

However that would be a trivial and costly thing to do. A more significant strategy would be to focus on the media, which would call for an imaginative selection of material or a revealing documentary film – or perhaps more than one. Using sport as the theme, such a presentation should demonstrate the constraints Third-World competitors face and how they transcend them. The presentation should neither brag nor play for pity, but calmly show how the apparent equality of opportunity offered by the games may be less than that because of the conditions under which Third-World contenders train. An athlete from a developing society has to achieve much more to reach the level of international competition; the presentation could emphasize the lack of adequate facilities for training, the nutritional deficiencies from which the entrants often suffer, the loss of face should they not live up to expectations and the ingenious use of the natural environment in their training. With a short, to-the-point commentary, it will make a strong impact on those who cavalierly assume that young people from the Third World make natural athletes, that a kind of genetic providence operates in their favour in the field.

Thus the message will be wider than the immediate subject, which is the games. For although its focus will be on the contestants, it will in fact deal with the cost of performance to humans in the conditions of underdevelopment. Such an approach, if well turned, can evoke not just respect but wonder.

When a competitor from a developing country wins an event, especially one like the marathon, the media spotlight is turned, at least momentarily, on his or her society. It is then that it becomes positively crucial to have suitable material ready at hand. At such times, diplomatic officers prove their worth if they are good at relating to media people or at appearing themselves on the media. They can quickly supply background, answer questions, correct misimpressions and draw out the implications of the achievement. The better the background or the more adroit the media performance, the greater will be the double impact – that of an athletic triumph supported by a media success.

It is of great utility to a developing country to send with the team at least one journalist who is expert but not myopic about sport. Such a person can put into vivid and memorable words for readers in the host country something of the flavour of the society whose team he accompanies. Most countries send journalists to report the event, especially those in which their competitors shine, back home. Well and good. But if the strategy is to turn the event into an education, those who accompany the team must write and speak for an audience wider than their own countrymen. Occasionally one finds in developing societies a poet or novelist with an eye for sporting events over and above the love of his own literary medium. To dispatch someone like that with the team is to get the best of three worlds: sound reporting on the games, a compelling description of the athletes' culture and the writer's literary impact.

The curiosity of the millions is always quickened by two powerful ingredients of any sports event: the mastery of physical form and the mystery of human personality. People who watch a spectacular race, for instance, whether in person or on television, are intrigued not just by the drama of it but by the individual performers; they see their temperaments, their styles and the foibles that give them their distinctiveness. At no other brief periods in the lives of nations (always excepting elections and revolutions) do personalities so seize the imagination as during international games. Writers will command readers everywhere if they can relate personality to performance, set the contestants within the contexts of their countries and show how they triumph over constricting circumstances.

Developing countries are at their weakest here, not because they lack literary talent, but because they have yet to recognize how that talent can serve a cause larger than sport. It is a weakness that they should immediately seek to rectify, especially as participation in world sporting events is something they consider of the highest importance. The media of the developed countries are as ubiquitous in sport as in politics, appreciating that the former appeals to far more people than the latter. Indeed when people think of international sport they think of radio and television; broadcasters, if not actually deciding the events, certainly decide how a large part of the public interprets them. Leading contestants are constantly interviewed by journalists of every sport. There is speculation before an event, there is analysis after it, and into both exercises not just the performers but their team officials are drawn. If the officials put on a poor show they rob a winner of some glory, they lose for their country some of its appeal and they take away from the world another viewpoint of itself.

An object lesson to the Third World on how to do it was provided by the Romanians at the 1976 Olympics in Montreal. Nadia Comanicchi, the almost boneless wonder of a gymnast, caused the spotlight to fall not just on her but on her country. Astonished experts and laypeople alike asked about the conditions in which she was raised and trained and the milieu that was responsible for them. Romanian Olympic and diplomatic officials, prudently sensing that their hour had come, firmly set the young lady's wondrous performance in the ideological and educational framework of their country. Without labouring the point, they demonstrated that socialism can be as fertile a matrix of physical flexibility as capitalism is reputed to be. They produced well-timed, well-turned material to establish the virtues of an educational system far different from those constructed on Western principles, and they caused many who had dismissed socialist norms to reappraise the capabilities of societies within the Warsaw Pact.

Some of the developing countries had competitors of like quality. Their performances too electrified Montreal, but only briefly. The adulation of the moment was not translated into a sustained admiration broadening into an intelligent openness to their societies. That resulted from the lack of seasoned communicators able to establish the relationship between excellence and circumstances, between challenge and response. The opportunities gained by superlative athletic performance were therefore lost by inadequate foresight.

All this imposes on developing countries a twofold obligation: to devise a clear strategy for participating in international, global or even sectoral games, and to choose skilled officials, some to provide the management and expertise the teams require, others to project the image their countries require.

Politics, these days, is never far below the surface of international sport whether at the Olympic heights or down in single-game events. But the politics of sport is more than arguments about what other nations should take part. Sport involves another important and highly productive aspect of politics – that of education.

Third-World contestants go to the stadium not just in quest of perfection, but in quest of understanding. They want those who have every training facility at their disposal to understand those who train with very little. Such an understanding will lead to conclusions about the way opportunities are distributed across the world. Interpretation is consequently as important to them as record-breaking and prize-winning.

What this calls for, in fact, is discussion and careful planning for the games at the highest levels at home, involving the ministries of foreign affairs, information and education and the public bodies responsible for organizing national sport and culture. In a number of developing countries this co-ordination is relatively easy, because the ministry responsible for sport is also responsible for information or culture. Even so, the tug-o-war over the selection of personnel to accompany the teams is bound to be fierce. Nor is it easy to strike a balance between the men and women who will manage the teams and those who will communicate with the public.

This is an exercise in relating policy to events. Political discipline is needed in small and poor Third-World countries as there is usually heavy pressure to increase the number of officials accompanying the teams. Bureaucracies of sport are like any other bureaucracy: they obey the fundamental law of self-justifying expansion. But when foreign currency and other resources are scarce, the selection of personnel to accompany the teams has to conform to the strategy adopted.

The selection of men and women is one thing. The selection of material is another. The men and women will return home. The material will remain behind in the mission to assist the diplomats turn excitement into recognition and recognition into awareness. Here the peculiar skills of the embassy personnel come into play. Much of the printed matter used to give enthusiasts advanced warning of coming talent will not be suitable for their continuing education after the event. In dealing with international sport, diplomats must remember three distinct stages, those before, during and after the event. I have already touched on the possible approach to the first two stages, which are characterized respectively by anticipation and excitement. The characteristic of the aftermath is exposure. A well-handled operation can take the curiosity of the pre-games period and the excitement during them and later mature them into intelligent interest and even sustained fascination.

Youth is to sport what experience is to politics (perhaps golf is an exception to this *mot*). So it is to the educational systems of the host country that the missions should reach out during the aftermath. Suitable material should be sent to primary, secondary and tertiary levels. To ensure the blessing of authority, mission staff should approach boards of education while post-game euphoria still disposes them to welcome the refreshing injection into their syllabuses of material not entirely local. The educators, having had brought to them the world, usually wish to keep it.

Helping them to keep it is the job of the Third-World diplomat. To do this, he must be sensitive to the culture and atmosphere of the host country and know what engages attention, what stimulates discussion, what promotes comparison and what engenders respect. The diplomat, obviously, cannot write the material himself. Most of it will have to be done at home, but his advice on selection, structure, colour and composition will make the difference between providing a learning experience sufficiently worthwhile to be repeated and an exercise in tedium.

In the case of the printed material, a first draft done at the embassy can be given colour, vividness, perspicuity and resonance by the professionals at headquarters. If a film is to be produced (an expensive proposition for a small developing country), it should be of such quality as to compel the attention of audiences, particularly young ones, in the society where the games were held. To do it badly is worse than not to do it at all.

The ambassador and his staff are vital to the production. Having observed what it was about the competitors that interested the spectators and commentators, they can guide the filmmakers to build the story from these aspects. The film will relate skill or speed to culture, culture to environment and environment to survival. It will smoothly interconnect the phases of the argument and convey the message of a world gone awry. Films made in this mould neither preach, which would render them dreary, nor propagandize, which would render them irritating.

If a country cannot afford films, then high-quality colour slides – never to be undervalued in their efficacy – can be a low-cost substitute. If they are selected carefully and supported by a skilful commentary, the audiences will identify with what is being shown and accept the implications of the presentation. Most missions mount photographic exhibitions during the games while there is virtually a captive market. A wise mission will also mount photographic exhibitions *after* the games when people, especially young ones, will have begun to sort out their impressions. Such a series of exhibitions, particularly at schools and colleges, where photography is often the art of self-discovery, will use the games as a point of departure for a journey into the heart and needs of a country.

In all of this, one thing should be remembered. Writers, film-makers and photographers are all people with an eye for the significant detail that resembles a well-turned epigram: memorable because of its form; inexhaustible because of its economy. This is the link between the artist at home and the diplomat in the field: both eschew (or should) heaviness of manner, both cultivate form and both are aware that impact is seldom achieved by gravity, that a lightness of style can imply sureness of touch.

Schools and colleges are crucial in the aftermath, but they do not form the mission's whole target. There are always mature persons impressed by individual competitors, and there will be sports commentators and officials wishing to continue their contacts and seeking information about the country and its culture. Not infrequently such individuals belong to organizations that can be interested in particular societies and will perhaps help to improve the sports facilities there or provide equipment. No less infrequently these individuals and groups see sport as a means of increasing amity among peoples and understanding among nations. Third-World missions that labour to assist these groups in their bridgebuilding will be doing construction work in the relationship between developed and developing worlds.

But all the activities demanded of diplomats from developing countries call for a level of training that at the moment is available in only some societies. The demands also call for new approaches to training that have not yet been energetically tackled. To the selection and training of Third-World diplomats we must now turn.

7 Preparing for Larger Purposes: the Selection and Training of Third-World Diplomats

If politics is the art of the possible, diplomacy is the art of taking the possible beyond its local dimensions. The instruments used in this process must be finely tuned, for what can be struck with broad notes at home must be done with consummate artistry outside. By its very nature politics is combative – and not less so in one-party states than in those described as parliamentary democracies. For men agreed on ends will differ as to means and men agreed on means will differ as to modalities. This is what gives the game its attraction and the practitioners their gusto. Aggression is the better part of valour.

The classic description of diplomacy is war carried on by different means. This may be true in some situations, but it is not the whole truth. It is often the diplomat's job to prove an identity of interest behind an apparent clash of positions; to look for ways of establishing that two sides have concealed common ground. Some apologists say of the diplomatic profession that the art of revelation stands highest with it. Revelation not in the sense of giving away secrets, but in the sense of discerning where the self-interest of parties converges, of unveiling the convergence to both sides and then of exploiting this mutual interest.

To equip a man or woman for this exercise in penetration, timing, synthesis and persuasion requires a carefully planned training programme. It is not that a diplomat always has to be subtle or oblique. There are times when straight talk is salutary. But the practitioner must be able to suit his approach to the occasion, the substance to his audience. For this he requires dis-

144

cernment, a quality he arrives at through experience and sensitivity. Sage selection and systematic preparation will ensure a diplomatic service a supply of officers imbued with these useful attributes. There are, of course, orthodox approaches to the selection and preparation of diplomats. But let us first examine the less-structured types of appointment.

In many developing countries, a few appointments to the higher echelons of the foreign service are made from the professional classes, people with extensive experience of public life who, competent within their own spheres, also have a flair for influencing thinking people in general. These are not political appointments in the classic sense. For although the appointees are not selected by the normal procedures, neither are they politicians, practising or retired. Such people can bring great strength to a foreign service.

Their appointment is less a reward for political services rendered than a recognition of talent; accordingly they can be expected to take to their postings a broad view of their functions, which they will discharge with flexibility, initiative and professional self-assurance. Having come to diplomacy from outside, they often have a restorative effect on their new colleagues, whom they will stimulate to look critically at erstwhile sacrosanct assumptions. Thus do they bring perceptions of methodology that established practitioners tend to overlook.

But that does not exhaust the catalogue of their usefulness. These men and women have not habitually exercised political power and have learned to get things done by persuasion, strategy and patience. They know the value of homework – much of it they do themselves – and they also know the danger of impulse and the need to stage-manage conditions so they are ripe for their policies or to adopt for their own purposes conditions created by others. Being disposed toward learning, they will come to diplomacy with a humility that is not diffidence. Their new profession, like their old ones, has valid procedures and acceptable shortcuts. This they will realize and approach diplomacy with critical but receptive minds – receptive because failure to master the game will put their own survival in doubt; critical because their professional and community experience has taught the value of comparison.

Such officers can speak with authority to their professional opposite numbers in the countries of their posting. They will be

heard with a respect that in turn usually matures into intimacy –
an indispensable asset for an ambassador or minister-counsellor,
especially as professionals in other fields tend unjustifiably to look
upon diplomats as masters of method but not of content.

If the general thesis of this study is accepted – that diplomats of
developing countries need to cultivate several constituencies in
developed societies – then mastery of content in professions
outside diplomacy implies substantial advantages, especially for
small countries.

A moment's comparison will show why. An ambassador or
senior diplomat of one developed country in the capital of
another will (unless relations are sour) carry authority – indeed,
his authority precedes him. Before he speaks, his audiences are
disposed to listen. Doors are opened without knocking. Even
should he be only moderately competent, his country's clout or
political closeness will ensure he can perform acceptably. The
mutual interests that bind the two countries together, touching at
many points, render the ambassador's task one of routine
lubrication.

It is different with the ambassador of the Third-World country
blessed neither with size nor coveted resources. Here it is his
personal authority and his acumen that will secure him a hearing.
To establish himself with the inner courts of the mandarinate and
among the large clusters of professionals and opinion-formers, he
needs a palpable grasp of many subjects. But if he is acknowledged as an expert in one area, even one unrelated to diplomacy,
he has a ready-made advantage that will enhance his diplomatic
performance.

Of course, such a diplomat cannot expect to establish his
authority immediately. He will give himself time to test the waters
and to be tested by them. But *psychologically*, the conviction that
in one domain he has a certain sovereignty will give him the confidence he needs. When he approaches those in the more rarefied
circles of diplomacy, they will respect his expertise and respond
with something better than courteous indifference.

Some politicians have taken to the job of ambassador and
joyously played the professionals off the field. But they are the
few. Most have failed to acquire diplomatic style, for obvious
reasons. As politicians, though not incapable of employing the
velvet glove, they would regard as unhealthy an obsession with
form and nuance. It was their word that ambassadors translated

into programme. Posting them abroad as ambassadors means this situation is reversed, which imposes a psychological burden. The tendency to continue acting as though they set policy rather than carry it out can be a travail for themselves and their countries.

Two dangers are inherent. First, his political Excellency may do nothing at all. Years of robust combativeness may have left him with little taste for learning the niceties of intergovernmental etiquette or the sophisticated skill of influencing opinion-formers. Understandably, his Excellency may interpret his appointment as a reward for services already rendered. He may conclude that presence, not performance, is the thing. But the great danger is that the erstwhile politician may try to do too much. Accustomed, at home, to being assured that his decisions will have quick results, he may dispense with the discreet plugging away which is essential for dialogue with cautious men and women.

Other people's bureaucracies seem, in particular to a new ex-minister, always to move more slowly than one's own. Attempts at hastening the process, especially by using the media, can and often do lead to accusations by the host government of interference. That means a barren tenure of office and a discomfited plenipotentiary. Small, poor, developing nations can afford neither ambassadors who do nothing nor those who clumsily do too much. In both cases the necessary increase in support staff is too costly. So also is the damage-limitation exercise that results from the efforts of an impatient amateur diplomat.

It takes great skill and greater sensitivity to jolly a bureaucracy to one's chosen goal, and politicians with these talents are too useful at home to be spared as heads of missions abroad. Those inconvenient at home are not likely to be made serviceable abroad by a change of air and honorifics.

Apart from the appointment of non-diplomatic professionals and political figures, most small and middle-sized Third-World countries habitually recruit young people who have been to university either at home, in the region or in the developed countries. They are never short of applicants. The diplomatic career in nearly every society has a glamour for both young and not-so-young. And as living conditions in many Third-World countries deteriorate, serving one's country overseas, especially in a developed society, is seen as having all the advantages of migration without the stigma. So it is not surprising that the foreign service ranks among a great many new graduates in arts

and social science as number one on the list of desirable
occupations.

Governments therefore have to ask themselves how best to
select and train new foreign-service officers to ensure the most
suitable types enter the service and are put to best use. Let us
first, then, look at what developing countries, particularly those
that are small and poor, want from their diplomats.

Both for personal effectiveness and the sheer survival of his
country and its kind, a Third-World diplomat must be able to
recognize the centres of real power in the country of his posting.
He must distinguish between those structures set forth on sancti-
fied paper and those operating in unsanctified fact. He must
decipher the hierarchies of decision making and gauge how the
channels of upward as well as downward communication work. If
he can discern the mechanisms that hold together the checks and
balances and see where the system tolerates disagreement and
where it demands unanimity, he will be earning his pay. And he
will earn his promotion when he can distinguish between
negotiable disputes and deep schisms, or between arguments over
emphasis and arguments over fundamentals. If he is able to
detect, before it becomes the conventional wisdom, decisive shifts
of interest or conviction in the country of his posting he will be of
immense value to his own. All this demands structured thought
and incisive analysis, a mind, suspicious of an apparent lack of
system, that seeks to dispel the semantic smokescreens common to
all those who manipulate the levers of power.

There is merit in having candidates write an examination, in
countries that have no shortage of graduates. An examination
tests the sense of structure – in conception, analysis and
expression. For diplomacy is a highly structured profession, and
its members must understand the hierarchy of rank. He who will
survive in it must appreciate the importance of subtle gradations.
Even more imperative, those who enter a foreign service must
recognize that the world a diplomat has to survey, interpret,
operate in and report on is a highly structured affair, in which
response must match the diplomatic environment. Candidates
with minds that do not easily boggle before complexity are what
the selectors look for, as are those who can discern the pattern
behind confused political or economic events. The examiners will
also welcome evidence that a candidate can view with scepticism
the mythology that large commercial enterprises use to disguise
their extent and influence.

The selectors will be wise, however, to avoid those who substitute ideology (whether of the right or the left) for rigorous analysis and who reduce any complex issue to starkly simplistic terms. These people, although often articulate, mistake dogmatism for dialectic. To misquote Lord Palmerston, they do not recognize that while a nation must have permanent principles, those principles do not have permanent applications.

When you come down to it, one of the most important functions of a diplomat is to keep his government informed precisely about the pivotal points of another country. Who controls what, and how much clout does he have? Which are the lovers' quarrels and which marriages of political convenience are about to be consumated or dissolved? Clearly, diplomats do not have the time to research these things as academics do; as I explained at the beginning of this book the necessary socializing in itself precludes this, not to mention the day-do-day nitty-gritty of an ambassador's life. The diplomat lives in a world of rapid if often circular movement, and his ability to detect structures is as much instinctive as cerebral. His skill is akin to that of a good investigative journalist, whose nose is an indispensable part of his equipment but who none the less would be untrue to his profession if his instinct was not married to a capacity for systematizing.

To decide whether a candidate has this uncommon combination of gifts, a conventional examination like that taken at university will be of little use. It is merely doing again what the university has already done – and done well. Further, a degree is no index to the qualities mentioned. A university examination does not make that sort of judgement, being concerned primarily with specialism. What is needed is another type of examination, one set in such a way as to ascertain whether the candidate has the required qualities. Such examinations are still rare in developing countries, one reason being that they are hard to set. They ask as much from the examiner as from the examinee. But assistance if needed can be readily obtained from an international body like the United Nations Educational, Scientific and Cultural Organization, only too willing to help in exercises of this sort, and for Commonwealth countries from the Commonwealth Secretariat. Alternatively, advice can be had from a developing country like India or Brazil that has perfected a system for the examination of recruits to its foreign service.

A system of written examinations followed by personality assessment has much to commend it. Diplomats spent much time writing reports, usually at speed and under pressure unless a mission is so heavily staffed that the workload of each officer is not heavy. But few non-oilbearing, small or middle-sized developing countries can afford that sort of establishment. Therefore a candidate for the foreign service must prove that writing clearly, succinctly, vigorously and *attractively* comes easily. What is written must command attention at the ministry, whose functionaries must get all they need to know in reports that go to the heart of the matter without a prefatory survey of the universe.

Written examinations reveal which candidates are likely to possess those requirements. But wise selectors will recognize that there are different types of communications skills. Working as they must on the principle that communication is one of the prime duties of diplomats, they will seek a balance between three types of skills. To the first type belong those as articulate in the spoken as in the written word. Not as rare as is often believed, they are of tremendous value to governments, because what they report home is authoritative enough to base decisions on and what they say in the host country impressive enough to command attention.

The second type comprises those with a flair for communicating with groups and audiences, think-tanks and task forces. These can make an interesting and memorable exposition of a grey report, one that may be full of formidable statistics. The third type embraces those whose skills lie in draftsmanship, who have the knack of framing compact yet comprehensive resolutions to provide each negotiating party with a compromise that it feels serves its interests. Not only should a balance between these types be preserved in the selection of recruits, but in the staffing of missions. Deciding who they are, however, takes the selector well beyond the written examination to other methods of assessment, of which I shall have more to say.

The foreign services of developing countries need a wide assortment of skills, which must of course be put to the best possible use. The skills required, to mention a few, include those of trade and commercial specialists, agronomists, various technologists, media experts and linguists. It will not be necessary to put one of each category at every mission, which would be too expensive. But in regions where a specific skill is required, a specialist can be attached to clusters of missions. He would report to all the mission heads but be under the immediate control of the most senior of them. The developed societies have long put a premium on the expertise of non-traditional types of officer in their main service and have expanded the attaché system to meet the changing requirements of diplomacy. Small developing countries cannot usually afford an extensive use of the attaché system, especially as effective attachés can be costly. If they are paid well and given a sufficient expense allowance, it would strain the budget, always inadequate, of the foreign ministry. If they are not, their personal embarrassment will seriously impair their effectiveness. This means, in effect, that poor countries usually depend on regular diplomatic officers to do what in the richer missions expert attachés do. The result is that much information relevant to the Third World is lost to the countries in question. The missions cannot make contact with technical or specialized bodies because they have no one who can speak to these institutions in their own jargon.

Any examination for entry to the foreign service of natural scientists, media people, technologists, engineers and agronomists should test ability to relate their discipline to the international scene. Third-World missions need expert opinion available to them to deal with many specialist problems – to cite just a few, there are the production and distribution of food in general and foods like cassava and rice in particular, the politics of pharmaceuticals, hydro, solar and nuclear power and their relationship to other forms of energy, the development uses of marine biology, the structure and functioning of international bodies like the World Health Organization, Food and Agriculture Organization and the UN Centre for Human Habitation (HABITAT) and the information problems of developed societies and the multinational organization of news coverage. In many of these areas, sadly, most Third-World missions are at the moment content to be coasting amateurs.

The important thing is to remove the impression, now nearly universal, that entry to the diplomatic world is reserved for those who have majored in subjects like law, economics, international affairs, political science and history. Certainly these graduates will gravitate to the diplomatic service and will for some time form the majority of its officers. But two factors are important here. The first is the effect that officers from the non-traditional disciplines will have. They will impart to their more traditional colleagues a broader consciousness and strengthen the mission's representation by making its use of scientific, technological, nutritional and informational material more competent and less easily contestable. Indeed in presenting their country's position at any of the routine forums, the confidence of conventional diplomats will be buttressed by a grasp of specialist subjects in which their expert colleagues have been able to advise them.

The second consideration is the contribution that officers trained in diplomacy, and whose specialities are scientific, technological, agricultural and chemical, can make at international conferences. For instance, conferences dealing with food production, water distribution, pollution, the ecology, energy and the like are as much diplomatic affairs as they are technical ones. They involve committees, rapporteurs and lobbying and demand skill in timing interventions, in drafting resolutions, in projecting widely agreeable positions as well as in the exhausting art of compromise. Technical personnel who have learned something of the moods, signals and modalities of the international milieu are vital as support staff to the topflight delegates from home. It also means a considerable financial saving for the government, as delegations do not have to be so enormous as to be unwieldly. In time, of course, the experience of such diplomatic officers will make them prime delegates in their own right.

At individual missions their value will quickly establish itself. Their disciplines will give them an entrée to circles closed to the purely diplomatic officer. The members of such circles are not only originators of specialist literature themselves, they also know where to find other literature of the same kind. Moreover, the verbal exchange of information and the rarefied gossip among their members are as useful to a Third-World diplomat as the published material. He will not only detect what is of use to his country, but he also knows how much of it to send home and exactly to whom.

What is revealed in print is seldom as crucial as what is not. Hence the above-noted, indispensable powers of detection and analysis are as vital to the specialist officer as to the more general practitioner. For instance, it is very important to have diplomats dotted over various regions of the developed world observing the multinationals – not just the political aspects of their behaviour, but the scientific and technological ones as well. Here the ability to follow the scent, as it were, is of paramount importance. The multinationals are distinguished for their ability to give away nothing – 'what they reveal is not worth concealing, and what they conceal is worth everything'. The scientific and technological diplomats will predictably concentrate on the direct effects on the economies of their own countries of the multinationals' activities. It would be prudent and professional to barter such information with similar officers of other developing nations. This would have the salutary effect of creating a wide Third-World awareness of the behaviour of the multinationals, which can be corroborated from other sources, notably the United Nations network.

The technological diplomat will also be a great blessing to the research bodies of his own country, eager for expert information on developments in rich societies. One of the routine functions of such diplomats is to protect their countries from purchasing expensive equipment totally unsuitable to local needs. Unfortunately, this happens often in Third-World societies. For instance, a piece of equipment may break down and must be replaced quickly to keep an essential service going. A team of officials – or perhaps just one man – sets off to the likely source and in haste purchases an unsuitable replacement. This is realized only after the contract has been signed, the debt incurred and the wrong equipment installed.

A diplomat with a technological background should be keeping his eye on the various kinds of equipment available that may be useful within his country. Even if he is not himself fully knowledgeable, he will be able through his contacts to get the required information quickly and make comparisons as to suitability and cost. He can see through 'disinterested' sales talk and read the fine print in the contracts. Such a diplomat will ensure that expensive blunders are kept to the minimum, thereby saving his country not only inconvenience and scarce currency, but also the international humiliation of being a sucker.

In most developed countries there are institutes to create and offer developing countries supposedly appropriate technology. Some of it can be useful; some is suitable for one environment but not for another. Some of it looks inexpensive but turns out to be the opposite in practice. Having an expert available to examine these offerings is a service Third-World nations can no longer afford to do without. The recommendations of such officers often vary considerably from, or flatly contradict, the assurances of those who sell the product. These officers can require modifications to make the product fully suitable for the conditions in their country. They can also assess the availability of spare parts and the speed of procuring them. Most important, they are there to ensure that a decision to purchase the product is based on a critical evaluation of its viability.

In addition to all this there exist in developed countries both an establishment technology network and a counter-establishment one. Those who belong to the latter are usually concerned with alternative, cheaper technologies, which they regard as less polluting and less prodigal of resources. The ventures and successes of the counter-establishment get little attention from orthodox publications and may be ignored by the mass media. But these experiments can be useful to societies that are struggling to marry technology to scarcity. A wise and well-trained technological diplomat will seek out members of the counter-establishment to learn their approaches, methods and techniques and transmit them to research councils and similar interested bodies at home. Few experts from home can afford the time or the money to cultivate such contacts or report intelligently on their successes and failures. The members of the counter-establishments are only too happy to make contact with diplomats who show an interest in their doings. But it is still necessary to study the question of whether their experiments can be sensibly applied elsewhere.

If Third-World countries are going to avail themselves of this kind of officer and really make use of his services, the selection process has to be comprehensive enough to make his candidacy possible. An examination that allows such people to demonstrate the required qualities from the starting point of their own disciplines will serve both the foreign ministry and the whole country well.

But a written examination is not enough – it may be a good guide to the candidates' minds, but it leaves undisclosed their temperaments and aptitudes, which are as fundamental to diplomacy as is pure intelligence. To learn about these takes the subtlety, sophistication and insight of senior members of the foreign service, with help from non-foreign-service panelists. One of these 'outsiders' could be a psychologist; the others should have a wide knowledge of men and women in public affairs, gleaned over years of experience.

Nor should the process be limited to one interview – a pathetically inadequate way of assessing personalities on whom so much will depend. Indeed, in a few developing countries, India for instance, candidates cannot be regarded as finally admitted to the foreign service – even after the most rigorous preliminary proceedings – until a probationary year has passed. Most small Third-World countries are too short of time, money and educated manpower to adopt so patient an approach. But some do not go far enough, simply allowing a cursory assessment to determine who will represent them abroad.

For best results and to ensure that those selected are of the calibre to mature, the candidates should be exposed to a series of situations, real or simulated, each designed to test different sides of their personalities. That might take a week or ten days. But it will be time well spent. Because countries with so much at stake cannot afford to be shortchanged by diplomatic officers ill-equipped to cope with the strains, constraints, temptations, seductions and the often-unadmitted boredom of diplomatic life.

After all, being an effective diplomat is one of the hardest professional achievements. Being an effective Third-World diplomat in a non-Third-World society is even harder. The work is often heavier than that of the average First-World ambassador because staffs are smaller. Projecting an image of his country, especially one that invites the reappraisal of rooted convictions, demands imagination, sensitivity, iron discipline, unfailing humour and stamina – qualities for which his colleagues from the older, richer states do not always have the same importunate need.

Even getting to know people of the host societies usually takes him longer. If the ambassador represents a country not much graced with the media's notice or noticed only to be damned, he usually has to work overtime to develop a web of contacts and friends. And the initiative usually has to come from him.

All the while he has to remain wonderfully beatific, gracious, urbane and accommodating, bearing his private strains with public insouciance and disguising his difficulties elegantly. To preserve that sort of equipoise requires sturdy inner resources, an imperturbable self-confidence and a mind as fertile in work as in play.

That last consideration is vital. Loneliness is an occupational hazard of diplomacy, visited at times on even the best of ambassadors, seldom for reasons that have anything to do with them as individuals. If they are men and women of absorbing hobbies, with major passions for minor pursuits (such as fishing, bird-watching, philately, jazz or miniature engineering), their isolation will be understandably irksome but is unlikely to be tragic. Naturally, the selectors will be on the lookout for those candidates whose varied interests enable them to amuse themselves.

On top of all that the ambassador must be a good mixer with an appetite for small talk and an almost clerical tolerance of platitudes. For diplomacy, more than most professions, is concerned with fleshing principles and policies. That means, in effect, negotiation, communication, persuasion.

Each of those three skills spells people. People at the top, inevitably, people in the middle increasingly and in the 1980s people whenever influence is exercised and opinions are moulded. An acceptable diplomat is one sound not only in assessing personalities, but also gregarious enough to enjoy them. The selectors will know that while the first talent matures with experience, the second is a matter of temperament.

Occasionally candidates with an indisputable genius for ideas and none for social interaction present a dilemma for the panel. Not to recruit them would be to impoverish the nation's role in international affairs. To post them abroad may be to do them little justice and their countries less. One way out is to reserve them for headquarters and international conferences, where the fertility and rapidity of their minds will greatly enhance their nation's cause.

Wise selectors naturally resist the temptation to choose those dazzling charmers who, though intellectually competent, are congenitally indisposed to toil and travail. They make of diplomacy a grand perpetual fiesta reminiscent of the glitter that surrounded the Congress of Vienna – splendidly anachronistic and bearing no relation to the realities of the countries they represent.

But that is not the only kind of candidate whom the selectors will have to resist. The hallmark of an astute diplomat is knowing how much information to reveal or conceal, when to reveal it, to whom and in what form. Veteran practitioners recognize that intelligence is no guarantee of discretion and that there are those whose egos need the boost of being the fount of confidential information. Highly impolitic as it is to send such people on overseas postings, it is barely prudent to retain them at headquarters even under the most vigilant supervision. But is takes more than one encounter between selectors and candidates to detect which of them are compulsive divulgers.

But it is just as important to identify candidates who cannot strike the balance between expounding and listening. Of course diplomats should be good talkers. But it is better for them to love the sound of their own voices less and the sound of other voices more. Listening is a highly rewarding discipline in a profession that, for the most part, lives by studied understatement. Few countries nowadays can afford the verbally incontinent officer long ago described by a sage as having a great determination of words to the mouth which precludes the reception of them by the ear. It is the sense of *timing* that make a diplomat both a good talker and a good listener. That is what the selectors are after in addition to self-control and adroitness in those social situations that will account for so many of their waking hours.

Observing them at cocktail parties, lunches or dinners, which the foreign ministry will host for that purpose, the selectors should have no difficulty in deciding on their social aptitudes. One thing will quickly reveal itself: which of the candidates can and which cannot hold their alcohol. Also which of them, being abstainers by religion or culture, lose nothing in conviviality thereby.

The guest list for these affairs should include senior officials of the foreign ministry itself, members of the diplomatic corps, local notabilities and recommendably a sprinkling of intelligent critics of the *status quo* offering alternatives to the prevailing political creed. These last will help the panel learn something of the intellectual balance of the candidates; those who talk only to the critics or only to the pillars of orthodoxy will have to be taught – if they are recruited – that in Western societies (particularly but not exclusively) the heretics and the orthodox may change places in power tomorrow.

To prepare candidates for the lack of reverence of the Fourth Estate in Western societies toward diplomats and to observe them under fire, they should be subjected to cross-examination by a seasoned journalist, one who is congenitally rude, hard-nosed, investigative and penetrating. The selectors can then observe which candidates have a quick grasp of a situation and its implications as well as the self-assurance and unflappability that blunt the pugnacity of such inquisitors.

Interviews with the electronic and print media may not be the day-to-day staple of a diplomat's life. None the less, he will have to face such challenges and he must at least be competent to do so. More common to his routine is the after-lunch or after-dinner speech explaining his country's policies to societies organized for political discussion. The sort of people attending such events are usually civil servants on their way to the top, political party intellectuals, senior business executives, columnists, correspondents and writers of books on international affairs. The sort of speech they expect is a thing of professional sophistication, a masterly blend of style and substance, suffused with personal authority. In short, a positive Waterloo for the unwary.

An ambassador's aim is to put his nation's point clearly and persuasively. What he says must be meaty but not heavy – good digestion and hard concentration do not go well together. Flashes of humour should come naturally out of what he is saying, which is much better than following the old and overworked formula of a witticism at the beginning and lugubrious solemnity thereafter.

This kind of performance demands research into the biases of the audience, arguments that are broadly based rather than tied to peculiar circumstance, and illuminating detail. Blessed are the brief, for they shall be invited again – better a half-hour speech and an hour's discussion than a one-hour speech and no discussion.

If the speaker can give to a carefully prepared text a conversational flavour, that guarantees a lively reception. He should especially seek a link between his own cause and his audience's interest. For instance, a Jamaican high commissioner to Canada might tell his audience (what they usually don't know) that the second wife of Sir John A. MacDonald, first prime minister and architect of the Canadian confederation, was a Jamaican. Or a Zambian ambassador to Washington might remind black congressmen that the African Methodist Episcopal Church contributed substantially to the education of the people who brought about the independence of Zambia. A Guyanese ambassador might tell East or West German audiences that one of their most distinguished explorers and cartographers, Robert Schomberg, helped to demarcate the boundaries of Guyana in the 1830s, besides cataloguing its flora, discovering waterfalls and writing about its society.

These historical examples, which are far more numerous than is generally supposed, will awake sympathy in the audiences. They can be uncovered by the history departments of Third-World universities. Third-World diplomats cannot afford to pass up such opportunities or to grasp them ineptly.

Using this linkage technique should, accordingly, be part of diplomatic training, and selectors should be alert to candidates who show evidence of being able to learn and use it well. Perhaps each aspirant could be required to deliver a short policy address to the panel and fellow-candidates based on simulated circumstances. This will show which candidates can be convincing and undisturbed by critical attention.

During training, the responsibility of developing these young people should not be that of the instructors alone. Local exemplars should be asked to share their skills, thus introducing variety and an exposure to different styles. Internationally minded lawyers (preferably adept at keeping their briefs short), technologists and scientists able to communicate in plain language, private- and public-sector managers and foreign-service veterans are suitable people.

Simulated situations are excellent tests of ability. The games must be planned with care, and they may well be based on actual negotiations in which the country has taken part. Some candidates could take the part of First and Second-World negotiators, others of Third-World personnel. Simulations are increasingly used in many forms of training, and in the present instance the technique may spread through the secondary and tertiary levels of education, a gain for developing countries.

Games of this kind will generate bargaining and an element of competition and inject excitement into the process – a healthy feature in a situation filled with nervous tension. Most important, the selectors will have ample evidence of the intuitive capabilities of candidates; thus they can round off their profiles of each one and admit the best to the training programme.

Once admitted to the training programme, the selectees will have to be as carefully instructed as they were selected. Some countries prefer on-the-job training, rotating the new diplomats to various desks for not less than a year each; they observe how the desk officers handle situations and use files, and they read dispatches from the missions and reports and resolutions of international and regional conferences and other relevant materials. As their knowledge increases they are encouraged to make recommendations for ensuing action. They also learn the routine of consular work and the legal tangles with which diplomats abroad have to deal, which are a far cry from the conceptual and strategic aspects of diplomacy.

This method of training is a distinctively British one, and when described on paper it sounds ideal and exportable. Indeed if a developing society has a foreign ministry like the British Foreign Office, a veritable bureaucratic cathedral, spacious, well-buttressed, splendidly interlocking, with the strains equitably distributed, then that form of apprenticeship falls easily into place.

But for the smaller and poorer developing countries those conditions hardly apply. Their problems are often shortage of staff, overwork, everests of files piled on desks, too few people chasing too many conferences, just enough time to hammer out strategies, not enough to teach trainees. That means the latter will be largely left without planned guidance on the backbone principles of their country's foreign policy and with very little demonstration of the methods that give them effect or of the complexities with which they have to deal.

The upshot is predictable. Cadets in the ministry set to work to teach themselves by reading reports, dispatches and files from which they try to abstract the conceptual and methodological tools of their trade. When they finally depart to their diplomatic destinations, their mental baggage consists of a miscellany of half-formed constructs, not a completed architecture. What they will certainly have acquired is a healthily unromantic view of the bureaucracy – valuable indeed as they ascend the promotion ladder, but not crucial enough for a sureness of footing abroad. In short they will go forth hard-boiled but half-baked.

Far more productive of sound and skilful diplomats is a training school. This school should be an entity distinct from the foreign ministry, though the two will, of course, be mutually reinforcing, both coming under the authority of the foreign minister. (Indeed, a diplomatic school that in addition to training foreign-service officers offers short courses also to civil servants and executives from other departments and corporations involved in international affairs will find itself in a good position when it comes to seeking funds. This in turn means an adequate expert staff and library – a gain to the whole country. Tanzania has taken this kind of initiative.)

The school, then, should be headed by a senior ambassador and manned by a small cadre of experienced diplomats whose teaching tenure should be not less than three years – about the length of a sensible posting abroad.

For the strictly analytic sections of the programme, the local or regional university could be asked to supply help – especially from its economics, political science and international affairs departments, plus those of history, sociology, modern languages and creative arts. The diplomatic instructors would have the duty of explaining the shaping of policy in the light of global, continental and regional situations, the strategies formulated to reverse unfavourable economic or political balances and translation of policy and strategy into day-to-day activity at the embassy level.

In smaller developing countries it is not usually easy to find scientific and technological experts who can relate their fields to the world of international politics for trainees. People like that are usually to be found within the United Nations agencies – especially UNESCO – and it seems likely that until the developing world creates its own pool of instructors, arrangements to have the UN agencies second suitable people to diplomatic training schools will continue. The contributions of UNESCO officials are especially vital to those countries that cannot afford to send their trainees to New York, Geneva, Rome, Nairobi and other headquarters to see these great organizations at work.

The school will obviously encourage visiting lecturers, especially ambassadors and minister-counsellors temporarily at home, senior ministry staff with specialized knowledge and, as mentioned above, seasoned communicators.

But to do this is not to exploit fully the reservoir of expertise. Many Third-World countries have been independent long enough that they have retired ambassadors and other senior diplomats, especially as in some of these states the retirement age is lower than in developed societies. Not to use the services of those willing to give them is to deny the trainees a wealth of distilled experience. Such people, now they are no longer under the pressures of the job, can shape the plenteous but unsystemized reflections of a long career into a structured body of thought, not omitting the lessons learned through mistakes, and highlighting important aspects of the political culture of various societies.

They have other boons to confer; they can offer advice on how to get the machinery at home to move at a pace satisfactory to those overseas – a skill often calling for the cunning of a Talleyrand and the resoluteness of a Gandhi – and they can point out the inobtrusive but powerful factors that shape foreign policy.

So how long should the training programme be?

Obviously, if it is not long enough to ensure a thorough training there is no point in having it. The new foreign-service officers it produces should be equipped to cope with the vagaries of the present international system without giving it their assent. They should also be ready for posting abroad in a matter of months. Well grounded in the interpretive techniques of their profession, they will be able to come to grips with a new political environment confidently, while only slightly suffering the discomforts of that unavoidable diplomatic malady: culture shock.

To this principle there is the limitation imposed by realism. The needs of foreign ministers for the services of recruits become more pressing every year, with the increase in international responsibilities of Third-World countries. A judicious balance has, therefore, to be struck between the claims of thoroughness and those of urgency. The classical Western academic year of nine months is too short in view of the range of topics to be covered and the depth at which they must be tackled. It is clearly inadequate for those studying one of the conventional diplomatic languages – English or French – and hopelessly impractical for those working on a second foreign language such as German or Chinese. Sixteen months would be ideal for all trainees, with the linguists allowed a few months extra. But a year and a third might put too great a strain on the patience of many foreign ministries. Training schools will probably have to settle for two months less than that. A prudent foreign ministry will, however, reconcile itself to fourteen months if as part of the programme the students spend the last three months working half of each week at various desks in the ministry and the other half completing their graduate essays.

These essays are worth considerable weight, both as the climax of the course and as the first substantial contributions of the trainees to the thinking that sustains foreign policy. Thus readership should not be restricted to the examiners; if students are enjoined to set down 16,000 to 20,000 words the chances are that seasoned diplomats will find the papers worth their time.

Each author would be expected to concentrate on one aspect of the country's international relations. He should analyse dispatches, mission reports, cabinet decisions, proceedings of ambassadors' conferences and other relevant material and recommend feasible strategies to improve the implementation of current policy. More fundamentally, some might document the inadequacies of the received wisdom in certain areas and suggest better alternatives.

Doing research is good. *Using* research is better. Students at the school should have available to them the essays of their predecessors, on which they can comment. This would expedite the learning process by showing students what is required of them. Outstanding essays (and outstanding dispatches from ambassadors) should be used as models on which students might pattern their own efforts.

A well-conceived, imaginatively taught training programme will leave students with the necessary self-assurance. It will have whetted their appetite for analysing structures and trends — always a matter of great satisfaction to young men and women. They will have been exposed to the intricate relationship between concept and practice — always a sobering experience for young men and women. They will have learned something about the difference between academically oriented analysis and policy-oriented analysis and the need for both. They will have learned to be sensibly aware of their own strengths and weaknesses. But most of all, they will have had time to relate the overview of foreign policy to day-to-day diplomatic activity and to learn the almost-intuitive art of shaping tactics and strategy. One lesson they should not leave their training courses without: how to respond to the often-formidable, immediate pressures without prejudice to their long-term foreign policy.

In view of all this, a good training programme will centre on two pivotal points around which others revolve. The two pivotal points on which, for the majority of Third-World states, the course will turn are international reconstruction and balanced and equitable national development. On these will hang all national preoccupations and diplomatic activity. Third-World diplomats in the next two decades will be emissaries of change, and their preparation for this role must have built into it a number of delicate balances.

The first of these is a balance between international and local knowledge. He who knows a great deal about his country but is hazy on the external structures that contain and constrain it will not have the penetration to promote his country's cause. Conversely, he who well understands the international scene but is hazy in his local knowledge will not have the credibility to be a good advocate. The Third-World diplomat in these times has therefore to unite clarity of thought and catholicity of knowledge. This is not easy, but it is now indispensable. His knowledge must be both of his own country and of the larger theatre in which he is performing. To it he must apply clear thought in a structured, disciplined and cogent way to give coherence to his actions and penetration to his reporting.

The second of these balances lies between an understanding of the present international economic, technological and informational orders and an understanding of the new orders the developing world wants to see in their place. The programme should set before the trainee diplomats the tenacity of the *status quo* and the necessity of change, so that he or she neither underestimates the powers against change nor undervalues the need for it.

The third balance the course must maintain is between analysis and practice, between the ornate architecture of a diplomat's job and the rude bags of cement and the dusty nuts, screws and bolts that constitute its fabric. The trainees must be conditioned to that curious juxtaposition – between banality, in the manifold trivia of each day, and the stimulation of high-level dialogue – that constitutes the opposite ends of the life he will lead.

A fourth balance is as compelling as it is often ignored: that between legal, political and commercial considerations and scientific and technological ones (including energy and agriculture). The course should emphasize that Third-World diplomats can no longer ignore these last. Those who did not study science and technology at university should at least be given selected instruction in them. It is not, to be sure, feasible to instil much technical knowledge, but the trainees should learn something of the relationship between science and the present international structures, and well as the changes in that relationship that would result from a restructuring of world orders.

If, as is here suggested, some of the trainees have a science background, there is an additional justification for the instructors to introduce the global aspects of subjects like energy, technology transfer, food distribution, the scientific policies of rich nations and the attempts of the poor nations to devise scientific policies of their own. Thus all students are exposed to these problems, and the insights generated among the students themselves will result in a cross-pollination of knowledge.

The final balance to be struck is that between conviction and sensitivity. The Third-World diplomat, as hinted above, has a job of conversion to do, pointing out to the thoughtful inhabitants of the developed world the self-destructive contradictions of their *status quo* and moving their minds to a broader conception of their own enlightened self-interest. But the style in which this is done has to take account of the cultural milieu in which the diplomat operates. He must know the taboos, implicit or explicit, of those to whom he will be addressing his message and the way of life in which their thinking and feeling takes place. If the Third-World diplomat is going to attack some of the sacred cows of the rich societies, he should be prepared to prove that they yield no milk and clutter up the road to economic growth. Doing these things demands a statesmanlike combination of what normally are incompatibles. To strike the delicate balance between burning conviction and dispassionate exposition calls for adroit timing and fine judgement. So high a degree of discipline is invaluable to have but difficult to acquire. Yet this is what the training course, to be of real use to the country or countries paying for it, must inculcate.

Clearly it will take rigour, discipline, resourcefulness and imagination to maintain these balances.

What follows in this section is not a suggested syllabus but a set of guidelines that may be useful in structuring or restructuring courses for diplomatic trainees. From these guidelines, different syllabuses, varying in accord with local or regional conditions, can be drawn up.

The starting point of the programme can be a thorough study either of the students' own country or of the present international orders. One can see advantages either way. To begin with a careful look at the geography, history, economic structure, political institutions, culture and outward perceptions of their society will anchor the trainees in a solid knowledge of that which they will spend their lives representing. Having deepened their knowledge and understanding of their own country, they can analyse and dissect the international environment in which it exists. The other approach has as much to be said for it and is the one I recommend. If the major obstacle to the balanced development of most Third-World countries is the present international economic order, then to analyse that order will to be initiate the trainees immediately into the perceptions they need and the responsibilities they will face.

They will come to have a clear understanding of what, as diplomats and as people, they are up against. They also will see exactly what it is they will have to set about changing. Most important of all, a prior study of the world's economic structure will give the study of their own country a deepened significance when they come to it. They will then rapidly perceive how much of the economic, social and political activity of their own society is affected, even frequently dictated, by those wide structures and how those structures impose constraints that have the effect of stultifying growth. The result is bound to be an increase in the global vision of the students.

A study of the present international economic order is of course essential. Primarily, students will analyse the agreements that brought it into being and now sustain it, along with its institutions, agencies, networks and trading patterns and the technology with which those who uphold it confirm their mastery. To equip the trainee to see the system in its multifaceted nature, the instruction will need to be interdisciplinary, although economics will be of first importance. That is not to say the course should be a hodgepodge of various disciplines. Those who plan the programme should carefully weave into a coherent whole the various threads of the system. The trainees, as they probe deeply into its day-to-day functioning, will learn of the system's interlocking nature.

If, as I have urged earlier in this chapter, the disciplines the students themselves bring are diverse, the interdisciplinary approach will not only call upon these wide resources, it will also make each trainee feel at home in the course. For he will see his own discipline as a tool of analysis and where it stops short, he will see how other disciplines take the analysis further.

What will be set before the students *à propos* the present international order? The emphasis will vary from country to country or region to region, but here are a few examples that every programme will use: the Bretton Woods agreement, the Marshall Plan, the International Monetary Fund, the division of the world into primary producers and industrial countries, the politics of food and energy, policies involving aid and agriculture, industrialization, technology transfer, the distribution of medical supplies and the use of the media to persuade vast populations not beneficiaries of the system that it is none the less inevitable.

As part of the study the rivalry of the superpowers will rank high, as will the elaborate minuets that keep that rivalry from developing into nuclear exasperation. This is necessary not only for an analysis of the international theatre but more appropriately (inasmuch as the terms of reference are Third-World perceptions of the prevailing system) to show the effects this rivalry has had and is having on the relationship between South and East, South and West not to mention South and South aid, trade and transfer of technology. A study of the Cold War and co-existence would be a prelude to analysis of the decade of *détente* and the effects of that decade on Third-World countries. And, as nuclear bluster is again in the air, careful attention should be paid to the recent relapse of the superpowers into binary antinomies – the new Cold-War Calvinism with its rigidities and its return to simplistic conceptions of orthodoxy.

All this can logically be followed by a close scrutiny of the contradictions of the present international economic order – contradictions leading to a weakening of the very economies it was intended to protect. In the study of contradictions the student will see the differences between the system's mythology and its actuality. The classic illustration of this is the concept of the free market and the erosion of that concept both by governments that profess to believe in it and corporations that exist to foster it – and this process is taking place during a steady slowdown of growth across the globe.

At this point the first pivot of the course is ready to be introduced: an intensive study of the country in which the training programme is taking place. It is as important to study its history (thematically of course) as it is to study its geography, agricultural system, industries, natural resources, demographics, political structure and processes and of course its political philosophy. Crucial too is its potential for development; if, for instance, there is a possibility of fossil oil deposits, balancing this with agriculture should be discussed. If there is no possibility of finding oil, the country's potential for developing renewable sources of energy should be looked at. The programme should also include a look at projects for increasing the self-sufficiency of the nation, including import substitution and internal distribution as well as of international marketing, and the constraints those attempts suffer. The political thrust to reduce or remove those constraints forms an important part of this section of the course.

Cultural diplomacy is an area in which many developing societies have shown a peculiar lack of interest. Part of the reason for this is that, though the diplomats themselves in their early and university education have been deeply immersed in the culture of their societies, diplomatic training has not emphasized the impact that can be made in rich societies by an imaginative presentation of aspects of it. The diplomatic training course should focus some of its attention on this facet of a diplomat's work. Models are available in which one or two countries have succeeded in portraying to developed societies both the concrete detail of the lives of many sectors of their people and its creative interpretation by various kinds of artists. Nor should the diplomat underplay the intellectual currents of his country, particularly the contribution of scholarly and imaginative minds. Yugoslavia is an excellent example. That country's diplomats have successfully explained the life, culture, creativity and self-image of the various nationalities within its borders. True, it is a European country, but in many respects it is more a developing society than it is one of the rich countries.

The course will move to a study of the region and of the country's relations with its neighbours, whether structural or bilateral. Next, a careful study should be made of regional institutions – their purposes and structure and the foreign-policy implications of their existence. If no such implications are visible, the students should consider the possibilities for a regional foreign policy.

From regional relationships and institutions the programme could easily move on to continental and hemispheric ones, such as the Organization for African Unity, the Organization of American States and the Association of South East Asian Nations. This, by widening the framework of interstate and interregional operations, brings the study back to the international orders and introduces the next phase, the move toward international reconstruction. Because this is fundamentally the study of change, some attention in the course should be paid to a cluster of disciplines few orthodox diplomats would normally consider relevant in such a programme. The social psychology of change, as mani-

fested in Europe and North America in the local political movements and international convulsions of the last hundred years
(more specifically in the last fifty), is a study that will endow the
trainees with the understanding necessary for persuasive representation in developed societies.

This will *not*, of course, involve a conventional history of those
regions in the nineteenth and twentieth centuries. Rather, it will
mean a thematic and interdisciplinary analysis of the politics of
pressure and the politics of compromise, a close look at how the
demands of the have-nots for a share in the benefits of the social
order were met and the devices by which their inclusion in the
power structure was made compatible with the continuing
primacy – though not supremacy – of the old ruling classes.

An even more productive experience for the recruits would be
to study how whole societies shifted from conflict between the
traditional old right and the old left to a broadly based, middle-
of-the-road consensus. They would analyse the nature of that
consensus – its mingling of social justice and social efficiency –
and the images and ideas on which it rests, images and ideas that
command the allegiance of the political, bureaucratic, mana-
gerial and labour directorates as well as the large mass of people.
In short the students would be observing the politics of mutual
convenience.

Of particular interest to them, in this connection, would be the
stages by which ideas once seen by the old ruling classes as con-
noting the doom of society (and by the deprived as too utopian to
be hoped for) have come to be regarded as commonsense – merely
the synonym for common acceptance – and even as com-
monplace.; This will lead them to reflect not only on how
political balance is achieved but how it is orchestrated. The
Scandinavian countries would rank high as examples for two good
reasons. First, they have proved particularly successful at
blending right and left. Second, their advanced programme in
development education and their contributions to development
assistance of 0.7% per cent of gross national product, as urged by
the United Nations, is evidence that they are sensitive to global
realities.

An analysis of decolonization would be inevitable in a programme of this kind, but not for the obvious reason that most
developing countries gained their sovereignty from that process.
The reason for giving it careful scruitny lies in the contrast

between the peaceful dismantlement of some empires and the bitter manner in which it was done in others. The purpose of the exercise would be to observe how the climate of acceptance at home was eventually created, how the loss of control over large chunks of land and property and millions of people was converted emotionally into a social gain, and how populations bred to the notion of empire as part of their national sovereignty and self-respect came to regard the whole concept as passé.

If the programme is well structured, one theme will never be far from the surface: the relationship between power and perception. In particular how was it that at certain junctures those who held power understood it must be shared and management broadened? The students would look at the sort of people, and where they stood in the social spectrum, who read the signs of the times aright and how they made their readings not just available but acceptable to those of their fellows accustomed to narrow interpretations of self-interest.

The theme of perception and power easily widens into one of perception and security. For security is both a political bedrock and a deep psychological need. Prescriptions for security vary from unchallengeable supremacy as its only guarantee to an environment of multiple alternatives as its most healthy one. There is no lack of case studies from the history of the last fifty years.

The unconventionality of that part of the programme in a diplomatic training institution will make its teaching by conventional instructors improbable. That does not make it impossible. This is just the sort of thing an organization like UNESCO would support – supplying the experts to tailor the programme and to teach it, particularly if the training institution is not a one-country affair but a regional effort, which would provide extra intellectual stimulus to the students.

Involving UNESCO clears the way logically and psychologically for study of the present motors of global change – the great international institutions through which the developing world is working to bring pressure on the rich East and West. These include the United Nations itself and its various committees, particularly the Group of 77. There are the agencies of the UN, such as UNESCO, the United Nations Environment Programme, the Economic Commission for Africa, the United Nations Children's Fund, the International Labour Organisation, World

Health Organization, Food and Agriculture Organization, United Nations Conference on Trade and Development and the Industrial Development Organization; plus the Non-Aligned Movement, the Commonwealth, the World Food Conference, the World Population Conference and the various specific mechanisms for the North–South dialogue. Attempts at South–South co-operation should get the attention they deserve and the students should be encouraged to propound their own plans for a secretariat of the South – increasingly seen as a need but not yet a fact.

Once the course has covered these crucial areas of orientation and analysis, other more traditional subjects of a diplomatic curriculum can be given – international law, diplomatic practice with its ramifications, consular practice and, inevitably, protocol.

To devise a training course of real value to small and middle-sized developing countries in the 1980s is well beyond the resources of single sovereignties. If the overriding factor is quality instruction rather than singularity, the training institutions should be regional or at least shared by neighbouring countries not uneasy about each other's ideologies. (Tanzania and Mozambique, for instance, jointly maintain an institution at Dar es Salaam.) The advantages are too obvious to detail. Certainly the range of skills and experiences offered to the students will be extensive and varied, with a judicious mix of practitioners and theoreticians. The conceptual ingredients of the profession are thus balanced with the day-to-day translation of them into practice – an experience that in turn nurtures its own forms of conceptualization.

But perhaps the most important advantage to be gained by having a regional training institution would be the evenness of quality of the graduates. In the eighties this has a profound significance. The Third-World chain is as strong as its weakest links. Small, very poor countries do not lack talent. But the talent often lacks training, so human resources are constrained by physical and geographic limitations. The discipline, exposure and stimulation that a good regional institution can provide will ensure even quality – and the costs to the more-favoured countries of the region would be no burden. The co-operation learned at a regional school will lead to an unlaboured cohesion when its graduates find themselves posted to the same country, and they will more smoothly synchronize their policies.

One observation remains to be made. It concerns the acquisition of certain skills. A regional training arrangement will allow for an exposure without which no Third-World diplomat should be sent to his posting. Each trainee should be allotted time in the editorial office of a newspaper and at a radio and television station. There is no better way to come to grips with the collective psychology of journalists and to learn how they perceive events and personalities, what they reckon to be a good story, how they filter the international scene into local consciousness and the relationship between what they want to say and what they think their employers or their audience will bear. All this will not only help to make the diplomats comfortable with the media, but also enable them as their experience grows to turn journalistic tenets to their own purposes. The rapport with journalists will stimulate the diplomat to continue learning about the arts of communication, which will improve his own effectiveness. As a bonus, he will acquire the small insights into eminent people that journalists love to trade among themselves.

If, as I have urged, Third-World diplomats have before them a major job of converting minds, there are three paramount attributes with which their training should imbue them: patience, wholeness and vision. With patience they can wait without frustration until the right time for action to make the best of their opportunities. Wholeness means being generalist enough to speak with authority and specialist enough to be an instrument of particular effectiveness. Vision enables them to see from their own countries and regions the world as a unity. Then the only international balance they will believe in will be that balance of opportunity that secures the earth from convulsion and gives to the poor the prospect of ending their deprivation.

Notes

1 S. de Gramont, *The French: Portrait of a People* (New York: Putnams, 1969).
2 S. S. Ramphal, *A World to Share: A Selection of the Speeches of the Commonwealth Secretary-General, 1975–1979* (London: Hutchinson, 1979).
3 W. Brandt, *North–South: A Programme for Survival*, Report of the Independent Commission for International Development Issues (Cambridge, Mass.: MIT Press, 1980).
4 There is a story that the president of a Third-World state telephoned his opposite number in a neighbouring country. 'My dear brother,' he said, 'can you lend me some communists? I am badly in need of Western aid.' 'I am so sorry,' replied the other president. 'I need all the communists I can lay my hands on, for just the same reason.' The story is not true; the moral is.
5 B. Davidson, *Africa in Modern History: The Search for a New Society* (London: Allen Lane, 1978).
6 Ramphal, *A World to Share*.
7 Mahbub ul Haq, *The Poverty Curtain: Choices for the Third World* (New York: Columbia University Press, 1976).
8 Pope Paul VI, quoted in S. S. Ramphal, *Kwame Nkrumah Memorial Lectures* (London: Third World Foundation, 1980).
9 Ramphal, *A World to Share*.
10 Ibid.
11 H. R. Trevor-Roper, quoted in B. Davidson, *Africa: History of a Continent* (London and New York: Spring Books, 1972).
12 Ramphal, *A World to Share*, p. 419.
13 'In politics, if you want anything said, ask a man; if you want anything *done*, ask a woman' – Margaret Thatcher, quoted by Anthony Sampson in *The Changing Anatomy of Britain* (London: Hodder & Stoughton, 1982) p. 34. True also of diplomacy, except that a well-trained female diplomat is often both a sayer and a doer.
14 Ambassadors who visit cities not on the itineraries of the celebrities usually find that whatever they say gets ample coverage. A wise envoy will relieve the local journalists of the bother of taking notes by supplying copies of his speeches – by far the most effective method of ensuring that the whole speech is quoted in the local press. If groups of Third-World ambassadors were to act in concert to visit the smaller cities of various regions in the host countries, the cumulative effect would be tremendous.
15 I. L. Head, *IDRC Reports*, 9(3) (1980) 13.
16 R. J. Snider, *Rich Christians in an Age of Hunger* (Downer's Grove, Ill.: IVCP Press, 1977).

17 Of course there is a division of opinion as to how to achieve this. The more right-wing Christians, like those who constitute the 'moral majority' in the United States, claim that contented people make for a more just world. The liberal and left-wing Christians say that just political and economic structures restrain the temptation to behave unjustly.

18 Witness, for instance, the immense Christian contribution to the European anti-nuclear movement, particularly in the Netherlands.

19 W. Brandt, *North–South*.

20 *Global Future: Time to Act: Report to the President on Global Resources, Environment and Population* (Washington, DC: US Government Printing Office, 1981).

21 G. O. Barney (ed.), *The Global 2000 Report: Entering the 21st Century. Report by the Council on Environmental Quality and Department of State* (Washington, DC: US Government Printing Office, 1981).

22 World Bank, *World Development Report, 1980* (Washington, DC, 1980).

Index